The Tottenham Outrage and Walthamstow Tram Chase

The Most Spectacular *Hot Pursuit* in History

Geoffrey Barton

Foreword Mike Waldren QPM

WATERSIDE PRESS

The Tottenham Outrage and Walthamstow Tram Chase
The Most Spectacular *Hot Pursuit* in History

ISBN 978-1-909976-40-5 (Paperback)
ISBN 978-1-910979-26-6 (Epub E-book)
ISBN 978-1-910979-27-3 (Adobe E-book)

Cover design © 2016 Waterside Press by www.gibgob.com Front cover image from an original in the possession of Waterside Press.

Printed by Lightning Source.

Main UK distributor Gardners Books, 1 Whittle Drive, Eastbourne, East Sussex, BN23 6QH. Tel: +44 (0)1323 521777; sales@gardners.com; www.gardners.com

North American distribution Ingram Book Company, One Ingram Blvd, La Vergne, TN 37086, USA. Tel: (+1) 615 793 5000; inquiry@ingramcontent.com

Cataloguing-In-Publication Data A catalogue record for this book can be obtained from the British Library.

e-book *The Tottenham Outrage and Walthamstow Tram Chase* is available as an ebook and also to subscribers of Ebrary, Ebsco, Myilibrary and Dawsonera.

Published 2017 by
Waterside Press Ltd
Sherfield Gables
Sherfield on Loddon, Hook
Hampshire RG27 0JG.

Telephone +44(0)1256 882250
Online catalogue WatersidePress.co.uk
Email enquiries@watersidepress.co.uk

Table of Contents

England Will Not Forget

(To the memory of Constable Tyler murdered in the execution of his duty)

Tramping up the last long beat
Comes a serried mass of blue
(Mournful roll of muffled drums)
Measured tread of many feet
All for what, and why, and who?
("For who?" cry the drums, "for who?")

Only a policeman, going home,
To the rest he has nobly won
(Mournful roll of muffled drums)
Only a humble man in blue,
Only a tale of duty done
("Well done" thrill the drums, "well done")

Only another hero's name
To add to England's roll of fame
(Triumphant rolling of the drums)
Only one of our very best
Going home to his well-earned rest
("To peace", sigh the drums, "and rest")

S J C

The Hackney and Kingsland Gazette
3 February 1909

On and Off Duty: Faithful Unto Death

(In memory of Constable Tyler, killed in the execution of his duty)

The day was dark and dreary
As we went on our way,
Past the spot where our comrade
Kept the assassins at bay.

He had gone at duty's bidding
Daring to do the right
Death facing without flinching
And foremost in the fight.

Comrade, we lay thee gently
Amid the flowers to rest.
Until the great awakening,
When the faithful will be blessed.

Gallant and brave was he ever
As many a time we saw,
And he saved the life of a woman
But a little while before.

And we pray that we, thy mourners,
May all inspired be,
To glorious deeds of duty,
Whene'er we think of thee.

Anon
1 March 1909

Acknowledgements

Abney Park Cemetery
All Saints' Church at Childs Hill
British Library (Newspaper Library at Colindale)
Embassy of France
Family Records Centre
The French Institute
Hackney Archives
Haringey Archives at Bruce Castle
Haringey Council re Tottenham Cemetery
London Metropolitan Archives
Meteorological Office at Bracknell in Berkshire
Metropolitan Police Heritage Centre
Metropolitan Police Museum at Charlton
Metropolitan Police Records Management Branch
Metropolitan Police (Tottenham Division)
National Archives at Kew
New Scotland Yard (Archives Department)
Southend Records Office
Vestry House Museum, Walthamstow
Waltham Forest Arts and Leisure Services
Walthamstow Central Library
Waltham Forest Cemetery

About the author

Geoffrey Barton is a skilled and experienced "thief taker." After joining the Metropolitan Police Service in 1975, he learnt his trade in Brixton and Walworth, where his size, strength and power soon singled him out as a fearsome adversary. He focused on professional street criminals, pickpockets, muggers and armed robbers. Having become a well-known and noticeable character on the streets of south London, he took to sitting in observation posts, identifying suspects to teams of surveillance officers who then followed them until they were about to commit or committed offences and were arrested. He was selected for firearms training and focused on tackling dangerous robbers and murderers including serial killers. He regularly arrested as many as ten suspects a day and on three occasions more than 50 in 24 hours.

The author of the Foreword

Mike Waldren QPM is the Historian to the Police Firearms Officers Association. Formerly a chief superintendent with the Metropolitan Police Service and now retired, he was Head of MPS Firearms Training and Operations.

Foreword by Mike Waldren QPM

Commentators largely see armed crime as being a post-World War Two phenomenon — with some justification. There were only ten armed robberies in London in 1951 but over the next 40 years this figure steadily increased to 2,789 by 1991 and there were similar rises throughout the rest of the country, although not on quite the same scale.

Police forces have adapted to deal with armed criminals and more recently with jihadist terrorists. However, back at the turn of the last century armed robbery was almost unknown and contingency plans to deal with what today would be called an "active shooter" out in the open were non-existent. This was because there had never been any need for them which is why an event in 1909 defied belief at the time and was almost immediately afterwards called "The Tottenham Outrage". Armed criminals, carrying "modern" firearms, which they were prepared to use, were chased through the streets over a distance of about six miles by police officers who were either unarmed or who were carrying firearms that were not only limited in number but out-of-date and badly in need of replacement.

They were joined by numerous members of the public, some of whom were also armed (which says a lot about the private ownership of firearms at the time), with a few of them even lending their guns to the police and showing a degree of "have-a-go" public spirit that would probably be considered out of place today.

Geoffrey Barton has made a careful study of the event and the story is told with commitment. More than that his book goes into considerable detail about the participants, the social conditions of the time and the aftermath. It is clear that in the absence of an armed response in the way that it is structured by police forces today, the officers involved did their best relying on guts and determination to see them through an unprecedented incident.

Mike Waldren QPM

To the brave police officers and citizens of Tottenham, Walthamstow and Chingford and to the memory of William Frederick Tyler and Ralph Joscelyne

CHAPTER 1

Latvia in 1909

Latvia is one of three Baltic states in Northern Europe, bordered by Estonia to the north, Lithuania to the south, Russia to the east, Belarus to the south-east, and by Sweden on its west along a maritime border. The climate is the same as that of its neighbour, Russia, generally very, very cold. It has a population of just over two million people, nearly 30 per cent of whom are Russian (some of whom have been declared non-citizens, with limited rights and no right to vote in national or municipal elections), and a territory of almost 65,000 square kilometres.

The country had been under foreign rule for six centuries before the First World War (1914–1918). The two great European powers that surround it, Russia and Germany, had taken it in turns with Sweden to rule the Latvians and it was only after the Germans had been defeated in the First World War and the Russians were involved in the Russian Revolution in 1917–18, that Latvia was able to establish its own independence and to form its own government in 1918.

Constant foreign domination led to resentment, frequent regime changes, uprisings and revolutions. It meant that the country failed to develop economically, politically, socially or culturally and that it had exceptionally large Russian and Jewish populations, as the Soviets attempted to integrate it into the new Soviet Union. In 1905 there was an attempted Russian Revolution that failed, but which triggered a series of events that led to many Latvians moving to London to work for Latvian independence, frequently relying on armed robbery as a means to raise funds to print literature which they then smuggled back into Latvia in order to secure support for their cause.

The First World War devastated the western extremity of the Russian Empire, including Latvia. Then, in 1917, the power vacuum created by the Russian Revolution coincided with demands for self-determination and autonomy and led to the Treaty of Brest-Litovsk between Russia and Germany in March 1918, which was followed by the Armistice with Germany on 11 November 1918. A week later, on 18 November 1918, the People's Council of Latvia proclaimed Latvian independence in Riga, with Kārlis Ulmanis becoming the head of the provisional government.

There then followed a generally chaotic period of civil unrest in Eastern Europe as many other countries took advantage of the power vacuum in Germany and Russia mentioned above to dispute borders that had been imposed on them by wars over several centuries. Having recently established its own independence and having a substantial border with the sea, Latvia had no current border disputes, but it did have a War of Independence. The chaos was however reflected in the fact that for a period in the spring of 1919, there were actually three Latvian governments — Ulmanis' government; the Latvian Soviet government led by Pēteris Stučka whose forces were supported by the Red Army and who occupied most of the country; and the Baltic German government of the United Baltic Duchy, headed by Andrievs Niedra and supported by the *Baltische Landeswehr* and the German *Freikorps* unit Iron Division. Clearly, although weakened, the Russians and Germans still sought to preserve their influence in Latvia.

Latvian forces then joined with the neighbouring Estonian forces to defeat the Germans at the Battle of Wenden in June 1919. The Latvians then focussed on clearing the country of the Red Army and, with the assistance of Polish troops (for whom the Battle of Daugavpils was a part of the Polish-Soviet War) eventually achieved this in early 1920.

A freely-elected Latvian assembly was finally convened on 1 May 1920, and adopted a liberal constitution, the *Satversme*, in February 1922. With most of Latvia's industrial base evacuated to the interior of Russia in 1915, radical land reform was the central political question for the new state. In 1897, 61.2 per cent of the rural population had been landless; by 1936, that percentage had been reduced to 18. By 1923, the extent of cultivated land surpassed the pre-war level. Innovation and rising productivity led to rapid growth of the economy, but it soon matched the rest of the world in suffering the effects of the Great Depression. By the end of its first parliamentary period, Latvia was showing signs of economic recovery, and had steadily moved towards the political centre.

Although many of these events occurred after 1909, they did not happen in isolation and they were, in fact, the culmination of preceding events over many centuries. They reflect, and explain the political situation that existed in Latvia at the start of the 20th-century and which spilled out onto the streets of London as robbery, running gun battles and murder between 1909 and 1911.

All change upsets some people; some people are not satisfied with the pace of change and some want more or want it to happen faster, and so it was that many Latvian Jews decided to leave Latvia, with a few sailing from Latvia to North America and, with most Latvians being fairly poor, many of them chose to move to London.

Immigrants Abroad

Immigrants arriving in a new country do not immediately spread themselves evenly over the whole of it. Leaving a country where your family is settled and established is a big step. People leave because there is a problem in the place where they are living. Only when they have decided to leave the country in which they are living do they give any consideration to where they want to live in the future and start to look for somewhere to settle, somewhere within easy, affordable reach and which they have heard is a good place. They frequently know little about their destination and settle near their initial point of landing, with family, friends and other people who have made the same journey, whilst they decide what to do next. This is why so many of the world's great cities have a Chinatown for example.

Since 1680 the areas of Houndsditch, Shoreditch, Spitalfields and Whitechapel in east London have been the initial destination for several groups of immigrants who have come to London to start a new life. These have included Huguenots, Jews and Bengalis. These people have found plentiful cheap housing and abundant unskilled work, so that they could settle here, feed their families and establish themselves in their new country whilst they decide on their next destination and their next career choice. Many of these groups stayed a few years before moving north to Tottenham, where they found better quality accommodation, still plentiful and improved employment opportunities and the chance to set up their own businesses. Frequently, these moves were prompted by the next wave of immigrants arriving in London.

Arriving in London speaking little English and with few friends, the Latvians must have been pleased to find a large population of Russian Jews already established in the East End of London. Seven years earlier, in 1900, a research project had shown that there were "well-defined intensely Jewish districts" where the concentration of Jewish immigrants had reached almost 100 per cent of the population. The Latvians slipped easily into their new lives and integrated with the Russians who shared their language, their politics and their religion, some of whom had been established in the area for nearly 30 years.

Nineteenth-century Russia had been home to about five million Jews, the largest Jewish community in the world at the time. Subjected to religious persecution and violent pogroms, many emigrated and between 1875 and 1914 around 150,000 arrived in England. The influx reached its peak in the late-1890s when large numbers of Jewish immigrants, mostly poor, either semi-skilled or unskilled, settled in the East End.

Some of the expatriates were revolutionaries, many of whom were unable to adapt to life in democratic London. The social historian William J Fishman writes that "the *meschuggena* [i.e. crazy] Anarchists were almost accepted as part of the East End landscape," although the terms "socialist" and "anarchist" had become confused in the minds of the British press, who used the terms interchangeably to refer to those with revolutionary beliefs. A leading article in *The Times* described the Whitechapel area as one that

". . . harbours some of the worst alien anarchists and criminals who seek our too hospitable shore. And these are the men who use the pistol and the knife."

Unrest Spreads Across Europe

The late 19-century had been a time of considerable unrest in Northern and Central Europe. There had been a number of wars and Russia and Germany had played an active role in most of them. As a consequence there had been substantial public investment in physical education and army cadet units so that young men learned discipline, drill and how to use weapons so that, on leaving school they provided a steady flow of outstanding recruits for the armed services. When these men grew disillusioned with the political situation in their own country they had come into conflict with the police and used their fitness and weapons skills to confront them. When they moved to London, they were unaware of Sir Robert Peel's attempts to democratise and liberalise the MPS and simply continued their armed confrontations with the police in England.

From the turn of the century, gang warfare persisted in the Whitechapel and Aldgate areas of London between groups of Bessarabia's and refugees from Odessa, and various revolutionary factions were active in the area. Robberies were often used as a tactic by revolutionary groups in Russia: the expropriation or theft of private property to fund radical activities.

The influx of émigrés and the rising rates of violent crime associated with it, led to popular concerns and comments in the press. The government passed the Aliens Act 1905 in an attempt to reduce immigration, but it was accused of failing to strictly enforce it; within a few years the Home Secretary, Winston Churchill submitted an amendment, which would have strengthened the Act, but he was persuaded not to follow through with it. The popular press reflected the opinions of many at the time; a leading article in the *Manchester Evening Chronicle* supported the Bill to bar "the dirty, destitute, diseased, verminous and criminal foreigner who dumps himself on our soil." In 2013, the journalist R⌐' Winder, in his examination of immigration into Britain, opine⌐ Act "gave official sanction to xenophobic reflexes which ⌐ remained dormant."

By 1910 Russian émigrés met regularly at the An⌐ Street, Stepney. Anarchism, derives from the C⌐ "anarkhos": "without a ruler"). It is an ideo.

20

political spectrum, which holds that societies should not have a government, laws, police or other systems of authority, but be based on a co-operative, consensual ethos. Contrary to what some may think, most anarchist theories imply an order of a strict, symmetrical variety, but it is emphasised that such order can be achieved through co-operation. It should not be confused with another belief called *nihilism* (from the Latin *nihil:* "nothing"), a purely negative and destructive activity directed against society. Anarchism is mostly a pacifist movement; however, there are radical anarchists who are prepared if necessary to use violence to achieve their ends. It was this search for co-operation that lead members to see religion as a problem, fearing that people would form relationships with God which would come between them working together as they believed they should.

A failed revolution in Tsarist Russia in 1905, followed by a number of other uprisings, had caused many people to flee from Russia and the Baltic states of Estonia, Latvia and Lithuania, many of whom poured into Britain as refugees. Some were escaping religious persecution, as Russia at that time could be a dangerous place for religious minorities, particularly Jews. The virulent anti-Semitism in some sectors of Russian society manifested itself in the notorious pogroms, when Jewish communities were, in that distasteful modern euphemism, 'ethnically cleansed' on a frequent basis. Others were revolutionaries, or members of dissident political groups, or people who were wanted in their own country for some misdemeanour or other.

We know far, far more about terrorism in today's world than people did in 1909, as it always seems to be in the news somewhere. But it is not a new phenomenon. We just hear more about it now because news travels faster, thanks to advances in telecommunications. In 1909, the influx of Russian dissidents caused panic and would lead to the Tottenham Outrage.

Despite its name, many of the Anarchist Club's members were not anarchists strictly speaking and the club's premises quickly became a meeting place and social venue for the Russian émigré diaspora, most of whom were Jewish. Indeed, the small group of Latvians who became involved in the events in Tottenham, Houndsditch and Sidney Street were not really anarchists at all, although anarchist literature was later found among their possessions. Members of the group were probably revolutionaries who had been radicalised by their experiences in their Russian homeland. All had extreme left-wing political views and believed that the expropriation of private property was a valid practice.

The probable leader of the group was George Gardstein, whose real name was likely to have been Poloski or Poolka, although he also used the aliases Garstin, Poloski, Poolka, Morountzeff, Mourimitz, Maurivitz, Milowitz, Morintz, Morin and Levi. Many club members appear to have been able to rival Gardstein with his 13 aliases and this made subsequent police enquiries quite difficult, as it was probably intended to do.

Gardstein, who probably was an anarchist, had been accused of murder and acts of terrorism in (it is believed Warsaw) in 1905 before his arrival in London. Another member of the group, Jacob (or Yakov) Peters, had been an agitator in Russia while in the army and later as a dockyard worker. He had served a term in prison for his activities and had been tortured by the removal of his fingernails. Yourka Dubof was another Russian agitator who had fled to England after being flogged by Cossacks. Fritz Svaars was a Latvian who had been arrested by the Russian authorities three times for terrorist offences, but escaped each time. He had travelled through the USA, where he undertook a series of robberies, before arriving in London in June 1910.

Another member was "Peter the Painter", a nickname for an unknown figure, possibly named Peter Piaktow (or Piatkov, Pjatkov or Piaktoff), or Janis Zhaklis. Bernard Porter, in a brief sketch in the *Dictionary of National Biography*, writes that no firm details are known of the anarchist's background and that "None of the ... biographical 'facts' about him ... is altogether reliable." William (or Joseph) Sokoloff (or Sokolow) was a Latvian who had been arrested in Riga in 1905 for murder and robbery before travelling to London. Another of the group's members was Karl Hoffman — whose real name was Alfred Dzircol — who had been involved in revolutionary and criminal activities for several years, including gun-running. In London he had practised as a decorator. John Rosen — real name John Zelin or Tzelin — came to London in 1909 from Riga and worked as a barber, while another member of the gang was Max Smoller, also known as Joe Levi and "Josef the Jew". He was wanted in his native Crimea for several jewel robberies.

Paul Helfeld and Jacob Lepidus

It was whilst pursuing the group's policy of expropriating private property in order to fund radical activities that two of the Latvians, Paul Helfeld and Jacob Lepidus came to commit the robbery in Tottenham in 1909 that is our story and two years later, in 1911, two other Latvians, George Gardstein and Jacob (or Yakov) Peters, to commit another robbery in Houndsditch that led to another famous gun battle with the police in London. This one was in the East End between a combined police and army force and two Latvians. Known as the Siege of Sidney Street or the "Battle of Stepney" it was the culmination of a series of events that began in December 1910, with an attempted jewellery robbery at Houndsditch in the City of London and it resulted in the murder of three policemen, the wounding of two more, and the death of George Gardstein, the leader of the Latvians.

As Helfeld and Lepidus died in the robbery in Tottenham it is not possible to investigate the rest of their lives in order to fully understand the type of people that they were but it is possible to look at the other Latvians who committed the Houndsditch Robbery and Siege of Sidney Street to get a better understanding of the people who were functioning in London around 1910.

One of the survivors of the Siege of Sidney Street was Jacob Peters. He returned to Russia, where he rose to be deputy head of the *Cheka*, the Soviet Secret Police, but was executed in Joseph Stalin's 1938 purge. Another survivor, Trassjonsky had a mental breakdown and was confined for a time at Colney Hatch Lunatic Asylum. Five others all disappeared shortly after Sidney Street, one in the USA, one in France, and three in London, possibly relying on the simple expedient of returning to their original names.

Both the government and the popular press recognised that there was a considerable benefit to be gained from pandering to the public view that the alien presence was unwelcome. This great animosity towards them was not new, and resentment had been smouldering for years. Therefore, in 1905, Parliament passed the Aliens Act, the first attempt in decades to stem the flow of immigrants arriving in England. The Act was mainly targeted at the recent flood of Russian Jews fleeing persecution in Tsarist Russia, but also covered other minorities.

The *Daily Mirror* of 27 January 1909 reported that, in 1908, 604 aliens had not been permitted to land and 356 others had been deported. The *Daily Mirror* of 30 January this same year went on to state that, in 1908, 171,000 persons of foreign birth arrived in the United Kingdom, an increase of 42,000 on 1907, but less than one per day had been deported and less than two per day had been refused admission. However, for the first time restrictions upon entry into this country had been imposed, and there was now a strong possibility of deportation for the criminal element.

Local historian, Deborah Hedgecock, curator of the Bruce Castle Museum in Tottenham says, "The outrage was particularly fuelled by the media. Lots of stories were being made up against immigrants who had moved into the area."

As we shall see in the book, over 1,000 local residents were prepared to take up cudgels and firearms to defend their way of life against the threats posed by the Latvians …

CHAPTER 2

Tottenham and Walthamstow Old and New

Tottenham lies within the London borough of Haringey in north London around eight miles/13 kilometres from Central London. Today it has a diverse and cosmopolitan population of some 130,000 residents. Over ten centuries old, it developed along the old Roman road called Ermine Street (part of the modern-day A10 trunk road). It lies between High Cross in the west and the River Lea (or Lee) and surrounding wetlands—known locally as "The Marshes"—in the east. Ever since the Lee Valley Regional Park Authority took over management of the area in 1972, nature and conservation has been a top priority (see generally, www.visitleevalley.org.uk/en/content/cms/nature/nature-reserve/tottenham-marshes/).

Tottenham's northern, western and southern boundaries are flexible and can be determined by bureaucrats as they see fit. But to the east the black hole that is The Marshes, separates it from Walthamstow so that its eastern boundary is fixed and unchanging. Nobody goes off the beaten track there in the normal course of events. If they do, they risk getting sucked down into the bowels of the earth and never being seen again. The Marshes are also filled with rivers, canals, streams and railway lines, all running north and south. As we shall see, two desperate robbers, having killed a policeman and a ten-year-old boy and who faced the death penalty if captured, had to swim river after river and clamber over railway line after railway line in their bid to avoid being captured.

Between Tudor times in the late-1500 to early 1600s and the Victorian era up to around the 1870s, Tottenham gradually became a desirable leisure and recreational destination for Londoners, particularly the better-off. Henry VIII visited Bruce Castle and hunted in Tottenham Wood.

A rural and somewhat idyllic Tottenham also featured in Izaak Walton's iconic work *The Compleat Angler*, published in 1653. The area became noted for its large Quaker population and its schools (including at Rowland Hill's at Bruce Castle). So, typically, it was a semi-rural, upper middle-class area until the Great Eastern Railway introduced workmen's trains and fares on its newly opened Enfield and Walthamstow branch lines in the late 1880s. Low-flung fields and market gardens were transformed into cheap housing for the lower middle-classes and working-classes, who were able to afford to commute to the Metropolis.

At the time, even the Metropolitan Police Service noticed and were affected by the scale of population growth. Senior officers reported that eight miles of new streets had appeared in the previous year with nearly 4,000 houses on them giving rise to consequent policing challenges. They thus sought additional manpower and resources from headquarters at Scotland Yard to deal with their changing territory. This book is best understood in the context of these vibrant but demanding changes.

Growth in population and the coming of the railways

As with many other towns and cities, Tottenham's (and London's) development was affected by the ever-increasing availability of (initially) steam trains to London and beyond. This growth is reflected in the following census statistics and information about local railway services:

1801	3,629
1811	4,771
1821	5,812
1831	6,937
1841	8,584
1851	9,120
1881	46,456
1891	97,174
1901	136,774

The Great Eastern Railway (already mentioned above) was not the only rail service to arrive in Tottenham. Others were:

- The Northern and Eastern Railway—Stratford to Broxbourne—opened in 1840 creating two stations: Tottenham and Marsh Lane;
- Tottenham & Hampstead Junction Railway opened in 1868, South Tottenham Station in 1871, two others, Harringey Park (Green Lanes) in 1880 and St Ann's Road in 1882 (but closed in 1942);
- The Stoke Newington & Edmonton Railway—the section between Stoke Newington and Lower Edmonton opened in 1872 with stations in Tottenham at Stamford Hill, Seven Sisters, Bruce Grove and White Hart Lane;
- The Palace Gates Line opened in 1878 with stations at Seven Sisters and West Green. Passenger services ceased in 1963, the line finally closing in 1965;
- Tottenham & Forest Gate Railway opened on 9 July 1894.
- London Underground's Piccadilly Line extension through Tottenham opened in 1932; and
- The first stretch of London Underground's Victoria Line opened in 1968 with a depot in Northumberland Park, as well as Seven Sisters and Tottenham Hale which with Bruce Grove, White Hart Lane and Northumberland Park also serve the area via London Overground.

Attractive to migrants

Shoreditch, an area east of the City of London, has a long-standing reputation as one of the first destinations and points of settlement for new immigrants to the United Kingdom. Close to their point of entry whether by dock or airport and the employment opportunities of the Metropolis, it also has (or had) plentiful affordable housing. Ambitious to make progress, immigrants tended to work hard and seek opportunities to improve themselves. Many then chose to make Tottenham their permanent home including when moving from Shoreditch.

Today, Tottenham has a distinctly multi-cultural population, with many widely differing ethnic groups. It contains one of the largest and most significant populations of African-Caribbean people. These were among the earliest immigrants to settle in the area, starting with the arrival of the first post-war West Indians in Britain on the *Empire Windrush* in the 1950s. Soon afterwards West Africans followed, notably many Ghanaians. Between 1980 and the present day there has been steady immigration of many others including Albanians, Kurds, Turkish-Cypriots, Irish, Poles and Zimbabweans. Tottenham is reported to be the most ethnically-diverse area in Europe, with up to 300 languages spoken routinely by its residents. David Lammy, the local MP, has suggested that nowadays Tottenham has the highest unemployment rate in London and the eighth highest in the United Kingdom, tied to some of the worst poverty rates in the country.

The ethnic make-up in Tottenham (2011) was as follows:

- 27.7 per cent Other White
- 26.7 per cent Black
- 22.3 per cent White British
- 10.7 per cent Asian
- 12.6 per cent Other/Mixed.

Broadwater Farm, Mark Duggan and other policing challenges

During the Second World War, Tottenham was hit by bombs in the first air raid on London (24 August 1940 in Elmar Road) and it continued to be a regular target until the end of the war, suffering V1 and V2 hits right up until March 1945. Since the war there have been major tensions between the African-Caribbean community and the police

On 6 October 1985 the Broadwater Farm housing estate in Tottenham was the scene of rioting following the death of Cynthia Jarrett, a resident of Tottenham who lived about a mile from the estate. She had died of heart failure after four policemen "burst" into her home to conduct a search. The response of the black community in Tottenham and the surrounding areas culminated in a riot beginning in Tottenham High Road and ending in the local Broadwater Farm Estate. Police Constable Keith Blakelock was murdered and 58 other police officers and 24 members of the public were injured in the fighting. Two of the policemen were injured by gunshots during the riot, the first time that firearms had been used in a disturbance in the United Kingdom in modern times.

The acknowledged tension between local black youths and the largely white MPS had been high due to a combination of local issues but had been triggered by riots in Brixton in south London which had taken place the previous week.

On 6 August 2011 at 8 p.m. in Tottenham High Road, two police cars, a bus, a Post Office and several local shops were attacked by youths and the police responded by sending public order teams to the scene and the second Tottenham Riot had started. Later in the evening it spread, with an Aldi supermarket and a branch of Allied Carpets also destroyed by fire. There was widespread looting in nearby Wood Green Shopping Centre and in the retail park at Tottenham Hale. Several flats above the shops on Tottenham High Road collapsed due to the fires. Twenty six flats above the Carpetright store in the Union Point development were also completely destroyed by fire. The trigger for this riot was later said to be a protest march by over 100 local residents against the death of Mark Duggan, aged 29, who had been shot by MPS officers assigned to Operation Trident two days earlier. The circumstances surrounding Duggan's death were not entirely clear at the time of the riot. On 17 August 2011, HRH Prince Charles, Prince of Wales and his wife Camilla, Duchess of Cornwall, visited an emergency centre to meet those affected.

In recent years there has been a considerable rise in the number of gangs and drug wars throughout Tottenham and the surrounding area, so that over the past three decades Tottenham has been one of the main hot spots for gangs and gun crime in the United Kingdom. These include the Tottenham Mandem Gang and various gangs from Hackney and the emergence of an organized crime ring known as the "Turkish Mafia" was said to have controlled more than 90 per cent of the United Kingdom's heroin market. In 1999, Tottenham was identified as one of the Yardies' strongholds in London, along with Stoke Newington, Harlesden, Lambeth and Brixton. Tottenham witnessed a high crime rate mostly related to drug dealers and gangs. The Tottenham Outrage in 1909 marks a transition from law-abiding, polite society to rebellious community struggling with both immigration and authority.

Some notable residents

Well-known people associated with Tottenham include:

- Adele Laurie Adkins ('Adele'), award winning singer-songwriter;
- Dave Clark, leader of the 1960s band The Dave Clark Five;
- Richard Hudson, singer-songwriter of The Strawbs;
- David Lammy (above) Labour MP for Tottenham since 2000;
- Ron Moody and Shani Wallis, actors, stars of the 1968 film *Oliver*;
- Leslie Phillips, actor;
- Lord David Triesman, ex-chair of the Football Association;
- Ted Willis, playwright, author of many acclaimed TV series, including BBC's *Dixon of Dock Green*; and
- Bob Bradbury, musician, lead singer of 1970s Glam Rock band Hello.

It is impossible to think about Tottenham without mentioning the town's Premier League football club and eight times winners of the FA Cup, Tottenham Hotspur. Founded in 1882, among many other honours "Spurs" have won the old First Division (now the Premier League) twice, the League Cup (now the English Football League (EFL) Cup) four times, the UEFA Cup Winners' Cup once and the UEFA Cup/League twice.

Walthamstow

Walthamstow is a town adjacent to Tottenham in north-east London, some 7.5 miles/12 kilometres from Central London. In 2011 it had a population of 109,424, which had been fairly static for half a century. It is bordered to the north by Chingford, to the south by Leyton and Leytonstone, to the east by the southern reaches of Epping Forest at Woodford and to the west by Tottenham and the River Lea. Leyton High Road, Hoe Street, Chingford Road, Chingford Mount (passing south-north through Walthamstow and its neighbouring towns) form part of an ancient route from London to Waltham Abbey (though seemingly not so historic as Tottenham's Roman road). It significantly increased in population as part of suburban growth and was incorporated as a borough in 1929 before becoming part of Greater London in 1965. Its growth is again reflected in the census statistics:

1871	10,692
1881	21,715
1891	46,346
1901	95,131
1911	124,580
1921	129,395
1931	132,972
1941	No census due to the Second World War
1951	121,135
1961	108,845

The railways and Walthamstow

With the advent of the railways and throughout the late 19th-century, Walthamstow experienced regular spurts in population and speculative building similar to that in Tottenham. Its Overground and Underground stations developed to include:

- Walthamstow Central Underground and National Rail station;
- Blackhorse Road Underground and National Rail station;
- Walthamstow Queen's Road;
- Wood Street;
- St James Street.

Protected (or isolated) according to points of view, by the River Lea on the west and Epping Forest on the east, Walthamstow comes over to the casual observer as a relatively more relaxed community than Tottenham. Nobody speaks of a local history of rioting, shootings, social disorder and crime. The town has a noticably middle-class core and is proud of its strong record of success in art, design, drama, music, sport and learning (as witnessed by the note of former residents at the end of this chapter). In some ways it feels like London's answer to Greenwich Village in New York. Although for many years Walthamstow had no local cinema, it did strangely enough have its own film studios.

The closest that Walthamstow ever seems to have come to experiencing a "riot" was in 2006–2007. The town has always been proud of its historic Central Library on the High Street, built with money donated by the Scottish-American businessman and philanthropist Andrew Carnegie (whose bust adorns the exterior of the building). In 2006–2007 it was expanded and modernised but there were claims that this was at the expense of book holdings. According to the *Waltham Forest Guardian*, "[A]lmost a quarter of a million books have gone missing from Waltham Forest libraries amid claims they have been burned or pulped," and the borough's library stock fell by 60 per cent over the two previous years. The residents of Walthamstow were outraged!

Walthamstow is also proud of its many connections to popular music, both as a location for singers and songwriters and in the words of a number of popular songs, for example Paul McCartney wrote the line "Long ago outside a chip shop in Walthamstow" in the Wings song *Old Siam, Sir* and Genesis referenced its lines of luxury cars in their music album *Selling England Pound by Pound*. Its street market (said to be the longest in Europe) and its history of light industry encompasses being a centre for the mass production of buses. The Marshes were once used for the launch and testing of light aircraft.

Notable residents

As mentioned above, Walthamstow has a strong artistic, musical, sporting and academic track record. Former residents include, William Morris, the artist and designer whose one-time home is now a museum dedicated to his achievements. The grounds are a public park, Lloyd Park close to Forest Road that features in our story along the route of the chase (see *Chapter 7*); and Frederick Bremer, the motor engineer, who launched the first petrol driven car in London in 1894 (nowadays on show in the Vestry House Museum). Clement Attlee, Prime Minister was the MP for Walthamstow throughout his premiershiership; and Benjamin Disraeli, Prime Minister, attended Higham Hall School. Baroness Scotland, Attorney General in David Cameron's Coalition government, was brought-up locally where she went to Walthamstow School for Girls.

Whilst Tottenham was a predominantly working-class area with a large immigrant population, struggling at various times in its history with maintaining authority and preventing crime, Walthamstow, the other side of The Marshes of our story, was and remains a relatively middle-class one, seemingly with greater time to focus on the arts and similar forms of recreation. William Morris apart, Walthamstow's thriving artistic community and artisans include (or have done so from time-to-time), such eminent people as Sir Peter Blake the artist; Sir George Edwards, designer of Concorde; Lucian Ercolani, founder of Ercol, the long-established and innovative furniture manufacturers; and 2003 Turner Prize winner Grayson Perry who had a studio in Walthamstow until 2014 (and renamed the town 'Awesomestow').

Modern-day actors or film-makers born or living in the area include Adam Woodyatt of the TV series *EastEnders*; Danniella Westbrook; directors Peter Greenaway (who attended Walthamstow College of Art); and Ken Russell (Walthamstow Technical College). Among the better-known musicians with local connections are jazz legend Johnny Dankworth (Sir George Monoux Grammar School: benefactor Monoux was Lord Mayor of London (1514) and founded almshouses in the town), and Ian Dury, singer-songwriter with The Blockheads (again Walthamstow College of Art).

At the risk of not mentioning the many other notables, but indicative of the area's diversity, others include people such as Tottenham Hotspur and England footballer Harry Kane (Chingford Grammar School), Air Marshal Sir Kenneth Charles Michael Giddings CB OBE DFC AFC and bar, born in Walthamstow in 1920, Anjem Choudary, the radical Islamist "preacher of hate" and former solicitor jailed in 2006, and Agnes Marshall, the culinary pioneer, who was born there in 1855.

CHAPTER 3

Tottenham Police Station

The Metropolitan Police Service (MPS)[1] nowadays covers an area of 1,578 square kilometres/609 square miles and a population of around eight million across London; despite frequent realignment of the borders these statistics have seldom changed significantly.

Traditionally, the MPS has divided London into around 25 territorial divisions, each responsible for an area of London roughly coinciding with the boundaries of a London borough and each assigned a letter of the alphabet as its name. In 1928, the closest date to The Outrage for which records currently exist, "N" Division had police stations in Goff's Oak, Cheshunt, Waltham Abbey, Enfield Highway, Chingford, Edmonton, Tottenham, Walthamstow, St Ann's Road, Lea Bridge Road, Stoke Newington, Highbury Vale and Islington. There were also other stations at Leyton and Leystonstone, which are close to Tottenham, but these were on "J" Division and there were few communications between police divisions in 1909 so it is unlikely that their officers would have been aware of The Outrage until they read about it in the newspapers the next day.

In 1990, the MPS decided to correlate its divisional boundaries by lining them up with those of the new London authorities, which caused some practical difficulties when officers had to travel through the territories of county forces to reach a few isolated residents, but which were considered less important than the political advantages of only having to coordinate with one local authority per division. Each police division tended to have four or five police stations within it, usually in the main/high streets of the largest towns. So there were approximately 120

---

1. For convenience, the term Metropolitan Police Service is used throughout this work even though, as noted in *Chapter 7*, it was formerly a "police force."

police stations in Greater London, or inside the M25 motorway. One such police station was in Tottenham.

Since 1990 the MPS has undertaken a re-development programme under which it has sold-off many of its older police station for them to become boutique hotels and blocks of flats, and has replaced them with out-of-town custody centres, built on remote industrial estates where the prisoners can be held "against a full-blown attack by the US Army," should that ever prove necessary.

Although many of the police stations that existed in 1990 were built before 1909, they were very different places to what they were later to become. The Victorian era was a time of great wealth and public servants confidently invested large sums of public money in vast stone edifices that they confidently expected to serve the community for centuries to come. Unfortunately, they were unable to predict many of the political, economic, cultural and social changes that would occur and with which the new buildings would have to deal. They also failed to predict the scientific improvements that led to the introduction of new technology.

Police Equipment Then and Now

Transport is a vital function for the police. Getting to and from scenes of crime as soon as possible, to the various courts on time, and keeping in touch with headquarters means that officers spend a lot of time on the move. In 1909 the police in Tottenham used horses, dogs and bicycles to travel around the division when they were in a hurry and when they were tired of walking. The dogs and horses could, of course, also he harnessed to carts to collect and deliver equipment or prisoner's property. There were no police motor vehicles at this time.

Six months after The Outrage, police superintendents, who had until that time relied on dog carts for their transport needs, complained to the commissioner that this was not in keeping with the dignity of their position and these were withdrawn. They were replaced by horse-drawn phaetons, light, four wheeled open carriages, which were, no doubt, far more in keeping, although not perhaps when it was raining, sleeting or snowing as it does so often in the winter in England!

The year 1886 is generally considered to mark the birth of the motor car, but it was only in 1908 when the Ford Motor Company produced the first mass-produced motor vehicle, the Model T Ford, that cars really started to become accessible to the public and it took several years to complete the process. In 1909 the motor car was still in its infancy, cars and vans were regularly seen on the roads, but they were generally owned by public utility companies, larger firms or by members of the aristocracy. Policemen are cautious people and at the start of the 20th-century their budgets were tight; they did not rush into car ownership.

In 1907, Metropolitan Police Commissioner Sir Edward Henry had been seen by the press outside Scotland Yard in a car. They took photos and asked questions, but were disappointed when they discovered that it was his own private motor vehicle. In 1911, Sir Edward decided that he really needed a company car and bought himself one; the next year, 1912, photographs of the car appeared in every national newspaper when he was shot standing next to it in an attempted assassination.

By mid-1920 the MPS owned six motor vehicles; one for the commissioner, one for the receiver (the chief financial officer of the MPS) and four despatch vans. The first operational vehicles, two Crossley tenders purchased from the Royal Flying Corps and known as "Flying Bedsteads", hit the roads in September 1920, and were quickly followed by two experimental wireless cars. It was considered essential to keep in constant touch with these new vehicles, so they were all fitted with Morse Code radios and operators who had served in the armed forces during the war were posted to them. The new squad of detectives who would use the Crossleys was called C8, the eighth department in the Criminal Investigation Department (CID) at Scotland Yard, but the aptly named crime reporter from the *Daily Mail*, W G T Crook, referred to them in his paper as the "Flying Squad", possibly due to the nickname of the Crossleys (above), or perhaps the speeds they achieved, 40 miles per hour!

In 1920, PC George "Jack" Frost, from "D" District was selected to become the first authorised driver of a police motor car when he was chosen from among 12 candidates to drive the Crossley Tenders for the Flying Squad, mainly due to his experience of driving the same vehicles during the war. In his book, entitled *Flying Squad*, published in 1948 he recalled that,

> "These Crossleys were big heavy vehicles with van-type bodies. The one which I drove most frequently carried the registration number XB 5706. They had no front wheel brakes, their tyres were very narrow, and they were difficult to hold at speed, or on wet roads; but they were very safe and powerful, as well as being extremely reliable."

Interestingly, four years earlier, in 1905, the *Police Review* reported that PC William Hallett from Tottenham had retired after 26 years as a mounted officer, and that it had been estimated that during his service he had ridden 144,000 miles, or more than five times around the world. (No details were supplied as to just how this had been calculated with no GPS or milometer attached to the horse!).

In 1909, Tottenham Police Station was not even equipped with a telephone, although Stoke Newington, as the divisional headquarters, was. Tottenham did have a teleprinter, which was a big cast iron desk with a built-in typewriter, attached to a telephone line, which allowed messages to be typed in at Tottenham and sent to the Scotland Yard Information Room, to other police stations, government departments, or companies owning a similar machine, where they would automatically be numbered and printed off, because the teleprinter had no screen. Effectively a teleprinter was a bit like email, but having no screen everything was paper-based. Today police officers use telephones, mobile telephones, fax machines and computers connected to the internet for their work. Given pads of paper and pens, and told not to use machines, they would be lost.

In 1914, at the start of the First World War, the Commissioner of the Metropolitan Police recorded in his memoirs that he had recently been away from his office when a telephone engineer had visited Scotland Yard. The engineer had been sent to instal a free telephone in order to allow senior officers to see their benefits and decide whether to rent or purchase any more for their other police stations. The sergeant at the front door of Scotland Yard, unsure of what he should do, eventually proposed that the new telephone should be fitted to the commissioner's private office, for his convenience. When he returned to his office and found the new telephone, the commissioner immediately ripped it out and threw it away. In his book he recounted this incident and commented that if he had kept it everybody would have been calling with frivolous complaints and problems, saying that he would never have got any work done. He declined to take any more telephones. Whilst his comments bore an element of truth, it is interesting to note that New Scotland Yard currently has something like 25,000 telephone, fax and internet lines, although it claims not to have enough police officers to respond to every call to a burglary or robbery. Perhaps the commissioner got it right in the first place!

The increased use of telephone, internet and fax improved communication with and within the police, provided a record of the messages received and sent and reduced the need for members of the public to actually visit the police station, so that today few people ever speak to a policeman or visit the police station unless they are stopped by an officer in relation to (usually) some minor offence. This has encouraged senior officers to build more police stations in remote locations, simply as communication hubs for electronic data and office space.

The police are the last resort when society breaks down and, as such, they frequently have to confront severe, potentially lethal violence. For this reason they need weapons. Each PC is issued with a wooden truncheon on appointment as a constable. For men, they are 19 inches/48 centimetres long and for women and CID officers they are 13 inches/33 centimetres long so that they are easier to conceal in handbags or pockets respectively.

In the early years the MPS also held stocks of cutlasses to be issued to officers on night duty. Although never provided for in regulations, common sense required that they were also issued in times of danger. Cutlasses were issued to police officers during The Outrage and many witnesses spoke of officers riding pedal cycles down the road with cutlasses either resting along the handlebars or being waved above their heads by officers both on foot or riding bicycles, as they pursued the killers.

Handcuffs, originally with a lock that required a key to close them or open them, but now with a fast self-locking mechanisms have always been popular with the police. Unfortunately, they have also been expensive so that instead of issuing these to all officers they were issued to the sergeant in charge of the police station who found that the safest way to protect them was to lock them into the firearms cabinet with the guns and keep the keys with him, so that the handcuffs, although held at the station, were seldom available when and where they were needed. Firearms were also held at all divisional police stations and this will be dealt with separately in the next chapter.

Recruitment and the Nature of Victorian Police Duties

In 1895, the MPS published fresh criteria for the selection of new recruits. These were that all recruits should:
- be over 21 and under 27 years-of-age;
- stand clear five feet nine inches without shoes or stockings;
- be able to read well, write legibly and have a fair knowledge of spelling;
- be generally intelligent; and
- be free from any bodily complaint. The bodily complaints for which candidates were rejected included; flat foot, stiffness of joints, narrow chest and deformities of the face.

Young men joining the police service therefore, were generally aged between 21 and 27 years-of-age and usually unmarried. When they graduated from the training school they were posted to stations in Westminster in Central London; those who were above six feet tall were sent to "A" Division, Cannon Row, Rochester Row and Gerald Row Police Stations, where they were employed to guard monuments near government offices. Those under six feet tall were sent to the other end of the city, to "C" Division, to West End Central, Vine Street and Bow Street Police Stations where they could police tourists in Soho, Mayfair and Covent Garden. They were then required to live in police section houses, which in those days were frequently contained on the upper floors of police stations. There was no sex before marriage in those days and young police officers could only marry after the necessary checks had been made on their proposed spouses and senior officers had given their formal consent in writing. When the officers finally were authorised to get married they were moved to semi-inner London divisions (a term used to signify those not completely central nor outlying, e.g. Walworth, Brixton and Islington) and supplied with police married quarters. Later, when they had children they were posted to Outer London divisions and the better off might consider seeking the approval of their senior officers to purchase property. This would only be granted after the necessary checks had been made on the new neighbours and the distance from the proposed address to the police station had been ascertained to fall within the regulations.

All this means that police station were generally quiet, restrained places, painted dark green or dark brown, illuminated by 40 watt light bulbs. Every day the same people walked around the station in silence. There were no cars or telephones and everybody, except the senior officers, was required by standing orders to use a "black writing ballpoint pen." And, of course, everybody was respectful of rank.

In 1909, every police officer was required to work 13 out of every 14 days. Officers were granted one weekly leave every second Sunday. In addition, each was granted ten days annual leave, but only when it suited the senior management. When not on duty, unmarried officers were required to continue to wear their uniform and to remain in the police station unless they sought and obtained the permission of a senior officer to visit family or friends, go to church, or out shopping. Officers who were off duty were clearly recognisable from those on duty because they would not be wearing a blue and white striped armband on their left forearm. Being in uniform in the police station meant that they could be called upon immediately in the event of an emergency, which, of course, was determined by a senior officer. In 1909, overtime did not attract any extra payment.

Officers in the section house were given a cubicle in which to live and sleep. It would have a screen to separate it from the next one. If more recruits arrived then the screens could be moved closer together. Each cubicle had a bed and a cabinet or cubicle in which the officer could place his uniform and personal belongings. Cubicles were checked frequently and no personal possessions were allowed to be outside the cubicle during an inspection, when the inside was checked for tidiness.

In 1909, the police station would have been considered something of a fortress. Few people visited it unless they or a close relative had been arrested and few were allowed to get much further than the front counter. Nobody who did not hold a warrant card and was therefore, at that time, white, Anglo-Saxon, heterosexual and Christian would have dared to try, or would probably ever have wanted to get inside the building. Most police officers based at the station would only have known the way to the locker room and the parade room. If the officer was ever summoned to see the superintendent to explain some misdemeanour, such as crossing the road to speak to the victim of a crime without authority (as he could have been at that time), he would have had to seek directions. Officers approaching the end of their service were allocated support roles, so there were no separate support staff. Police work was seen as work for policemen and there was no co-operation with solicitors and social workers. Forensic science was an unnecessary expense that took money out of the pockets of policemen. Better to "knock confessions out of prisoners," as this was felt at that time to be more reliable.

As already mentioned, ordinary policemen used black writing using ball point pens. This was because they tended to make their notes in rain, sleet and snow, holding a pocket book in their hand, frequently at an angle or against a wall. Only inspectors used fountain pens because they were allowed to work inside the police station and they didn't make blots on the paper. Only superintendents and above used red pens so that readers could immediately see what the final decision was without reading all the conflicting recommendations.

Early Intelligence of an Industrial Dispute

On Friday 28 January 1909, the day before The Outrage, information had been received at Tottenham Police Station that there was to be an industrial dispute in Tottenham Hale. This would have been reported to Superintendent Jenkins, whose responsibility it would have been to ensure that there was an adequate and appropriate police response to this incident. The demonstration would have required the selected officers to parade for duty at 6 a.m. No doubt Jenkins tasked one of his sergeants or inspectors to select officers for the duty and make any necessary arrangements for their transport and refreshment. An Operation Order would have been typed up, usually with two fingers, and the officers warned of their change of duty. Due to the early start, efforts would have been made to select only non-drinking officers for this event.

Those selected for the duty would have been awoken at 5 a.m. to give them time to press their uniforms, polish their boots, shower, shave, have breakfast and dress by 6 a.m., ready for work. Efforts would have been made to minimise the disturbance to the sleeping officers, although if they had enjoyed a good drink the night before this may not have been too much of a problem. With so many officers engaged at the industrial dispute at 9.30 a.m. most, if not all, of the remaining officers would have been "dragged from their pits" and told to prepare themselves for work on the market patrol at 10.30 a.m.

Shots Amid the Morning Chaos

Suddenly there were two shots outside in the street! Some of the officers would have been in the shower, covered in soap or shampoo, others would be half dressed, maybe still wearing their pyjamas under their uniforms, or wearing shirts without collars or with collars attached at the back but not at the front, or with their faces covered in shaving foam as they started to shave. Some would have been wearing one boot and trying to find the other. Maybe they were looking for a shoe horn to get the second one on as it was too tight.

Everybody ran out of the building, most by the doors, some went out of the windows; nobody wanted to be caught by one of the sergeants or inspectors as that would have been a disciplinary offence. Few excuses would have been accepted for dallying rather than assisting a fellow police officer being threatened with a gun. First out the door were PCs Tyler and Newman. Next, PCs Bond and Fraiser jumped out of a window and ran down the road. Many others followed ...

CHAPTER 4

Weapons and Training

Perhaps the most surprising aspect of the entire Tottenham Outrage and Walthamstow Tram Chase was the ease with which the local population produced a range of firearms and ammunition within a few minutes of the robbers firing off their first round. As the MPS were totally unable to produce their first firearm for more than half-an-hour and before that were compelled to rely on their truncheons and a few police cutlasses, this was probably just as well. Estimates of the number or weapons produced during the subsequent chase hover around 200, ranging from shotguns, rifles, pistols and revolvers, all loaded with the appropriate ammunition. These weapons would have been collected whilst on active service overseas with the British Army, or whilst on some overseas holiday and brought back through customs, without comment.

Before the Second World War, the United Kingdom Parliament focussed on passing laws to punish citizens who committed specific offences such as murder, robbery or theft. A good example of this type of legislation is the Offences Against the Person Act 1861 which made various levels of assault an offence and set out a number of criminal offences ranging from common assault, through actual bodily harm (ABH) to grievous bodily harm (GBH). Murder itself has always been a common law rather than a statutory offence other than in relation to sentencing or what are known as "partial defences", whilst manslaughter is a form of homicide less than murder (or "reduced" from murder due, e.g. to diminished responsibility) as a result of a range of statutory provisions. The chief effect is a practical one in that murder attracts a mandatory life sentence (until 1965 onwards capital punishment) and manslaughter a maximum and discretionary life term (only in the mists of time did manslaughter lead to possible execution). What is clear is that the murders during The Outrage would have fallen well within the nature of capital crimes even after the passing of the Homicide Act 1957 when sentence of death was restricted to certain types of killing: they included murder by shooting, killing a police officer acting in the execution of his or her duty (or anyone assisting them), when resisting arrest, double murder or murder in the course or furtherance of theft. So the perpetrators of The Outrage would have come within at least five of the categories of murder later deemed by Parliament to be of the most heinous kind. The following sections of the 1861 Act are key to offences of violence:

Sections 1–3.	Sentence for Murder;
Section 4.	Conspiring or Soliciting to Commit Murder;
Section 5.	Manslaughter;
Section 18.	Wounding with Intent to do Grievous Bodily Harm;
Section 20.	Wounding (Aka "malicious wounding");
Section 42.	Common Assault or Battery;
Section 47.	Assault Occasioning Actual Bodily Harm;

The Act also specified that assaults on certain types of individual would attract special punishment, including clergymen, magistrates and peace officers.

Crime Prevention

In the second half of the 20th-century, Parliament started to introduce preventative legislation, which rather than just penalising criminal acts, attempted to try and stop them from occurring, such as by making the possession of weapons and ammunition an offence or by giving police officers the authority to separate opposing groups who were likely to fight. Some legal experts take the view that, by 1909, Parliament had passed 14 Acts relating to firearms in the previous 750 years. A brief review of these Acts shows that most of them related to hunting game and controlling poaching, i.e. the:

1. Assizes of Arms of 1181 and 1252;
2. 1508 Act forbidding the use of guns or crossbows without Royal Letters Patent;
3. 1515 "Acte Avoidyng Shoting in Crossebowes and Gonnes";
4. 1542 Act introducing hunting licen[c]es;
5. 1549 Act forbidding the use of birdshot;
6. Bill of Rights 1689;
7. Disarming Acts of 1716 and 1725;
8. Act of Proscription 1746;
9. Vagrancy Act 1824 under which there could be an arrest of anyone "… armed with any gun, pistol, hanger, cutlass, bludgeon, or other offensive weapon, or having upon him [or her] any instrument, with intent to commit any felonious Act";
10. Night Poaching Act 1828;
11. Game Act 1831;
12. Night Poaching Act 1844;
13. Poaching Prevention Act 1862;
14. Gun Licence Act 1870;
15. Pistols Act 1903.

Some experts take the view that the first *real* Act to truly relate to firearms was the Gun Licence Act 1870 (No. 14 above). This stated that:

"Every person who shall use or carry a gun, or other firearm, elsewhere than in a dwelling house or curtilage thereof, without having in force a licence duly granted under this Act [available at any post office at a cost of ten shillings: 50 new pence] shall forfeit the sum of ten pounds."

An exemption was provided for "any person in the naval, military, or volunteer service of Her Majesty, or in the constabulary or other police force, using or carrying any gun in the performance of his duty, or when engaged in target practice." This was intended purely as a revenue measure to raise "the necessary supplies to defray Your Majesty's [Queen Victoria's] public expenses."

The final Act of Parliament relating to firearms before The Outrage was the Pistols Act 1903 (No. 15 above), which regulated the sale and use of pistols and is generally considered to be the first substantive attempt at "gun control" in Great Britain. It required the purchaser of a pistol to either hold a gun or game licence granted under the Gun Licence Act 1870 or, being a householder, to use such pistol only in his own house or within the curtilage thereof, or to proceed abroad for a period of not less than six months. It became illegal to sell a pistol to someone who was drunk or of unsound mind.

It is interesting to note that the MPS appears to have failed to notice the passage of this legislation and to inform its officers of it in Police Orders in the usual way, at least not until 18 months had passed. It is also highly unlikely that the police went around after The Outrage to check that all the people from whom they had borrowed guns actually had a gun licence under the 1870 Act allowing them to carry one outside "a dwelling house or curtilage thereof."

1920 Onwards...

It was not until ten years after The Outrage that the next Act of Parliament relating to firearms was passed. The Firearms Act 1920 required that any person having in his or her possession, using or carrying a firearm (excluding shotguns) obtain a firearms certificate. There was the usual exemption for police, military, navy and air service personnel on duty. A gun licence (under the Gun Licence Act 1870) was also still required to carry a gun elsewhere than in a dwelling house or the curtilage thereof. The passing of the 1920 Act was motivated, in part, by fears of a possible surge in crime due to the large number of firearms brought home from the First World War and fears of working-class unrest at this time. "An Act to amend the law relating to firearms and other weapons and ammunition," its main stated aim was to enable the government to control the overseas arms trade and so fulfil its commitment to the Paris Arms Convention of 1919. Shootings of police by militant groups in Ireland may also have been a factor, as Britain and Ireland were at that time still in union with each other and the Act applied there also.

The 1920 Act required anyone wanting to purchase or possess a firearm or ammunition to obtain a firearm certificate. The certificate, which lasted for three years, specified not only the firearm involved but also the amount of ammunition the holder could buy or possess. Local chief constables decided who could obtain a certificate and had the power to exclude anyone of "intemperate habits" or "unsound mind" or anyone considered "… for any reason unfitted to be trusted with firearms." Applicants for certificates also had to convince the police that they had a good reason for needing a certificate. The law did not affect smooth-bore guns, which were available for purchase without any form of paperwork. The penalty for violating the 1920 Act was a fine of up to £50 or "imprisonment with or without hard labour for a term not exceeding three months," or both.

The right of individuals to bear arms had previously been, in the words of the 1689 Bill of Rights, "allowed by law." The 1920 Act made this right conditional upon the approval of the Home Secretary and the police. A series of classified Home Office directives defined for the benefit of chief constables what constituted good reason to grant a certificate and originally included self-defence. However, the Firearms Act 1920 did nothing to prevent criminals from obtaining firearms illegally or using a gun in the commission of a crime and this was finally prevented by the Firearms and Imitation Firearms (Criminal Use) Act 1933, which imposed a penalty up to 14 years' imprisonment for anyone who might "attempt to make use" of any firearm or imitation firearm to resist arrest.

This legislative situation meant that in 1909 there were no real restrictions on citizens possessing, owning, carrying, supplying, importing or exporting any type or number of firearms or ammunition. The Pistols Act 1903 had been passed by Parliament in an attempt to curtail the use of pistols, but it took the MPS 18 months to notice its passing and probably even longer to consider how it should be enforced.

The people who owned weapons at this time were not generally criminals, but rather law abiding former members of the armed forces, or respectable middle-class people who could afford foreign holidays. It would cause all sorts of problems to go round with search warrants "kicking in the front doors" of these people's homes. The fact that 200 people were sufficiently confident to go home to collect their weapons, to stand shoulder to shoulder with their local police exchanging shots with the robbers with no fear of prosecution, to loan their weapons to the police confident that they would, in due course, be returned without comment or criminal charges, confirms this.

Firearms Training ... and Mishaps

By 1901 the MPS was having difficulty in sustaining its limited firearms training programme. Most of the sergeant instructors had been either promoted or retired and the annual range practice was often supervised by any officer of any rank who had military experience. Of course, unless these former soldiers had been officers, their army experience of firearms would probably have been limited to rifles rather than revolvers. In compliance with the original Police Order, the revolver (a Webley gate-loader model) was still loaded by the officer in charge of the training session and then passed to the next firer. He, in turn, stepped forward, fired his six rounds and handed the weapon back to be unloaded and reloaded.

But firearms and untrained men are a lethal combination and so it proved for "R" Division on 31 October 1901. A group of police officers at the Ammunition Works in East Greenwich were being coached by PC 577 "R" Walton, who had served seven years with the colours before joining the force in 1894. PC Walton showed the class how to aim and fire, but miscounted the rounds and fired five instead of six. He stepped back from the firing point and, as he began to unload, the sixth round fired. The bullet passed through the left thigh of one of his colleagues, PC Farley, and struck the left knee of a second officer, PC Reed.

On the same afternoon another group of sergeants and constables from the same division, supervised by sub-divisional Inspector Lee, were assembled at the Gravel Pits in Bexley Road in Eltham. Police seargeant 16 "R" Macdougall completed his practice, but also made the fatal mistake, literally, of firing only five rounds, instead of six. He handed the weapon to another sergeant, who began to unload; two empty cases which had been ejected when the sixth round was fired. The bullet struck Madougall under the jaw and shattered his spine; he died two days later in the Cottage Hospital in Egham.

It was not that these officers had difficulty counting when they ran out of fingers or toes to help them. The fact was that many of these officers had been selected for training with firearms due to their previous military experience several years earlier and with a range of different weapons. Until fairly recently, many of the older weapons had held just five rounds in the cylinder and the Army had taught soldiers to count their shots and re-load after five shots so that they could continue to defend themselves. The failure of the police to set up a new training programme meant that nobody had identified the problem and re-trained these men to count up to six instead of five. This had meant that weapons had been handed over between officers, with a live round under the hammer. This would not have been a problem, in itself, except that the design and maintenance of the weapons meant that, in certain circumstances they could be fired without pressure being applied to the trigger. With a gate load revolver, as the name implies, it was necessary to operate a small gate at the rear of the cylinder before the gun could be loaded. Pushing the loading gate to one side exposed one of the six chambers in the cylinder, but it was still essential to thumb the hammer back halfway. The last action locked the hammer in the half-cock position and disengaged a stop, thus allowing the cylinder to be manually rotated. Each chamber could then be loaded, one at a time, through the loading gate aperture.

In order to unload, the hammer was again drawn back to the half-cock position and the gate opened. Empty cartridges were then ejected singly through the gate aperture by means of the ejector rod; this swing-out rod was housed in the cylinder spindle when not in use. Apparently, no one had realised that, if a particular component in the mechanism was worn, it could allow the hammer to disengage from the half-cock position and fall forward. If this happened when a chambered live round was in line with the firing pin the revolver would fire, without any pressure on the trigger. This may well have been the cause of the two accidents involving "R" Division personnel, although there is nothing in the records to suggest that the two revolvers in question were ever stripped or examined to confirm or deny this possibility.

Superintendent Wakeford of "R" Division reported the two shootings to Assistant Commissioner Howard, who roundly blamed the range officers for lack of supervision and Superintendent Wakeford himself for appointing them in the first place. It is unclear at this time just what experience Howard had of firearms and on which he was basing his judgement. Clearly, he would not have wanted to accept the blame for the failure to set up an effective firearms training programme, for the selection of unsuitable weapons, or for failing to ensure adequate maintenance of those weapons himself, and would therefore have to look elsewhere for a culprit to blame.

On 2 November 1901, Howard sent a memorandum to all divisional superintendents asking for their suggestions on future safety precautions at the annual firing practices. Their replies, with few exceptions, were generally unhelpful and included one from the superintendent at Vine Street that blanks be used instead of live ammunition, which is not an ideal method of checking the officer's accuracy!

One of the exceptions, of course, was from Superintendent Wakeford who questioned every aspect of police firearms training and particularly the instructions that obliged untrained sergeants to load, issue and unload revolvers when parading reliefs. He also suggested that all live firing be conducted on a properly constructed range, the person in charge to be qualified and a scoring system instituted to ensure that each man fired all six rounds in the weapon. Finally, that all divisional revolvers should be used in rotation, in case any were defective. This last recommendation is vital. When the same officers are issuing and returning weapons on a daily basis, such as for routine VIP protection, it is not unusual for the officer using the weapon to have a favourite and seek it out every day. Similarly, the issuing officer can get into the habit of handing out bullets from the same end of the packet every day and then putting them back the same way, so that the self-same ones are issued every day. When I served on the Diplomatic Protection Group the officers did this and, out of 500 rounds of ammunition, 300 were worn out, and 200 were as new. The worn out rounds were dented and scratched, the bullet was coming away from the case and all the coating had fallen off.

Today, all these recommendations would be considered good practice and would be followed unthinkingly by all concerned. At the start of the century it was considered unnecessary. Views get distorted when the weapons are never used operationally.

The end product of these deliberations was a two page Police Order entitled "Revolver Target Practice" which was published on 18 July 1902. A firer was now permitted to load and unload his own revolver on the range, provided that he was personally supervised by a chief inspector or inspector in charge. Furthermore, "A careful count is to be kept of the shots fired by each individual" and any defective round should be withdrawn "with great care at the firing point, while holding the revolver facing the target." There were also seven common sense safety regulations, for example, "(e) No man will handle his weapon on the range except when standing in position at the firing point." In addition, each recruit (or candidate as he was then known) before being posted to a division was to be instructed "as to the manner of using and handling a revolver". A supply of revolvers and a quantity of drill rounds was to be supplied to the Preparatory Class for that purpose.

As the prospective range officers were as inexperienced as the men being supervised, the Police Order also included a complete drill sequence for handling a gate-load revolver. These instructions were reasonably explicit as is shown by the section on loading (below). The breech is, in fact, the loading gate.

"On the word 'Ready': Seize the pistol with the right hand , unbutton the pouch with the left, draw the pistol from the belt and pass it to the left hand, holding it nearly upright with the forefinger outside the trigger guard and half-cock with the right hand. Open the breech with the forefinger and thumb of the right hand, take the cartridges from the pouch (holding them by the rim) with the forefinger and thumb of the right hand, place one in each chamber, pressing them well home with the thumb, revolving the cylinder at the same time with the forefinger of the left hand, and close the breech. Full cock, and hold the pistol with the right hand, keeping it upright, with the forefinger outside the trigger guard. Drop the left hand to the side."

It should be remembered that in 1900 doctors estimated that one per cent of the population were left-handed; today that proportion is eleven per cent and still rising, as less pressure is applied to young people to conform and use their right hands. Somebody must have been left-handed, but no mention was made of the possibility. Pressurising a left-handed man to do things right-handed leads to accidents, as the brain will not be able to cope with the change.

In the other sections much of the shooting technique is at variance with modern thinking and at one point the instruction advocates keeping the eye fixed on the target instead of the sights. At least proper emphasis was placed on safe handling, however, and the firing drills were certainly no worse than those employed by the military. The drills were apparently taken from a report submitted 18 years previously by a "T" Division PC, appropriately named Alfred Gunns, based on his earlier experience in the Royal Navy. His original notes include a section on double action shooting (firing without first cocking the hammer) which he describes as a firing practice with the left hand, but six rounds per man per annum hardly ran to this type of training.

Sir Edward Henry Takes Over at the MPS

Colonel Bradford retired on 4 March 1903 and was succeeded as commissioner by Sir Edward Henry, who was soon to be embroiled in Superintendent Wakeford's campaign for a modern revolver. In 1903 the Dockyard Police were issued with Webley Mark IV revolvers supplied through the Naval Ordnance Department. The Mark IV was made with a hinged frame and depressing a stirrup catch exposed all six chambers; thus the weapon could be loaded, and unloaded without placing the hammer in the half-cock position.

Meanwhile the rest of the force was still armed with the 1884 issue of the gate load revolver. Wakeford, who was determined to prove that the accidents to his men had been the result of faulty weapons and not carelessness (he was probably right), refused to accept any revolver unless it was perfect. He continually returned them for repair and when replacements were received most of those were sent back as faulty. In particular he refused a revolver if the cylinder could be moved (indicating a worn stop) with the hammer down. Furthermore, a cylinder which was liable to shift (known in the trade as over-rotation) meant that a chamber could be misaligned with both the firing pin and the bore of the barrel. In the first case the pin might strike other than squarely on the cartridge cap (a misfire) and in the second, a sliver of bullet would shave off and fly sideways (side splash) as it was forced into the bore by the force of the charge. Nearly all the weapons in store suffered from one or more of these defects.

On 27 September 1904 the receiver asked the commissioner for directions and Sir Edward Henry examined one of the suspect weapons. He replied on 9 October that, "The Superintendent seems to be perfectly right and the sad experience in his division justifies him in being especially careful." The receiver was directed to seek expert advice from the Royal Small Arms Factory at Enfield, but instead he approached Boss and Company, a firm of gunsmiths at 5 St James's Street. In their opinion a small number of weapons needed extensive repairs, but the majority, despite worn cylinder stops, were quite safe to fire. The receiver passed this information to the commissioner adding that, "He will therefore be glad if the necessary instructions may be given to the Superintendent of 'R' Division." (Presumably an attempt to stop Wakeford condemning almost every service revolver that came his way).

Sir Edward, however, in a written reply, pointed out the danger of faulty revolvers, the importance of responsible advice, and asked the receiver to comply with his initial request. Accordingly, two revolvers were sent to the Army Inspection Department in Enfield Lock, where a Captain Pollard disagreed with Boss and Company. In addition to minor repairs, he recommended that each revolver be fitted with a second cylinder stop and a rebounding hammer. The latter has a small piece of metal welded to the base of the hammer, which forces the pin to move back, or rebound, away from the cartridge cap once the trigger is released. Thus, even if the hammer accidentally falls, or is knocked forward, the gun will not fire unless the trigger is squeezed at the same time.

The cost of converting all the force revolvers in this way was estimated to be £474 (about £43,000 at today's prices) and as the receiver considered that the Home Office would not approve this expenditure, only 324 weapons were withdrawn for refitting. While these revolvers were being collected it was found that only 663 revolvers could be accounted for on divisions or in store, instead of the 677 shown on the receiver's records. A thorough search was ordered, which revealed that six revolvers were with the recruits' class and that another five were with the Executive Branch, which left just three outstanding. So many weapons had been transferred for "Special Duties", returned for servicing, replaced from store or borrowed from neighbouring divisions, that there was no possibility of the missing three being found. Finally, on 5 October 1905, the force was obliged to admit that it had lost three revolvers. "N" Division, for example, listed 33 revolvers, which also agreed with the receiver's records, but managed to return 46. The worst offender was Scotland Yard, which had been issued with 27 revolvers, but which returned 68 to store whilst retaining another 25!

Range training was suspended during the conversion period, but by the end of 1905 a total of 345 converted Webleys had been issued and divisions resumed the annual firing practice. Another 25 weapons were later fitted with a rebounding hammer, but the fate of the 304 unconverted gate-load revolvers is not known. They were probably left to sit in a locked cupboard somewhere out of sight.

Regulations concerning training and the issue of revolvers remained unchanged and in fact were republished in a Police Order of 27 April 1906. This order also belatedly informed the force about a new Pistols Act which had been law since 1903! Although the 1903 Act provided a few minor controls, at least it was made an offence to sell firearms to the mentally-disordered or to anyone under 18 years-of-age.

Throughout its history. The MPS has pursued a policy of holding a total of around 1,000 weapons and of buying them as a job lot at a discount from a British supplier if at all possible. The Webley .450 calibre gate-load revolvers available at this time had been purchased a quarter of a century earlier in 1884 and were basically an English-made version of the weapons used by cowboys in the Wild West. There is no information as to whether anybody took the trouble to check the ammunition, which tends to deteriorate more quickly.

A survey by Assistant Commissioner Major (later Sir) Frederick Wodehouse in 1908 found that few, if any, officers were actually applying to be issued with firearms on night duty any longer and he therefore recommended that the number of weapons available to officers be reduced in order to save money. The commissioner, Sir Edward Henry concurred.

A few days after the robbery, the Home Secretary, Mr Herbert Gladstone declared the incident a riot under the Riot Act. This was, in effect, an admission that the government had failed to enforce the King's Peace and that as a consequence they were responsible for all the damages incurred by any citizen as a result of their failure. Opening the cash registers in this way encouraged every budding entrepreneur to consider the ways in which he or she had suffered financially so that they could submit a claim and make some money.

Ten days after the robbery on 2 February 1909, Sir Edward Henry set up a board to examine and report on the various claims for compensation being submitted by members of the public who had suffered as a result of the incident, regardless of whether they were the victims of it or taken part in the pursuit. The next day he added, "I should be glad if this board would also make enquiry as to whether our Service Revolver is quite suitable or whether it could with advantage be replaced by some other type. They should also report whether the numbers at present attached to each station is adequate."

The board consisted of two chief constables, Major EHT Parsons and Colonel Edwards, together with Superintendent James Olive. They carried out trials at the grounds of the gun maker, William Evans, at a total cost of £1 10s (£1.50). Despite the obvious urgency and although the board reported in March that the Webley revolvers should be withdrawn and replaced with "Colt Automatic Pistols," probably the Model 1903 in .32 calibre, nothing happened.

Whilst the board deliberated, two superintendents made representations to it. Superintendent Quinn of Special Branch was increasingly uneasy about the ten .45 Webley Bulldog revolvers which were the only weapons available for his officers "when engaged on protection or other duties." These were all that remained of 12 such weapons which had been purchased for the CID back in 1882, during the Fenian troubles (Those involving agitators seeking self-rule for Ireland). Quinn sought the advice of a Mr Churchill, a gunsmith of 8, Agar Street, who told him that his revolvers were out-of-date and quite worthless. In Mr Churchill's opinion, "they would be a positive danger in a melee as, except at very close quarters, their shooting could not be depended on." He did, however, offer to buy them for 4 shillings (20 pence) each provided that he supplied the replacements. By the end of the month Quinn had spoken to the commissioner who authorised the purchase of two Colt "automatic pocket pistols" at a cost of £3 3 shillings (£3.15p) each. At the same time, Superintendent Jenkins of "N" Division suggested that instead of two revolvers at each station there should be six, of a modern design.

The lack of action on replacing the firearms was probably a result of informal complaints made to the government by British firearms manufacturers, at the loss of a valuable order to a foreign rival. The fact that the decision had been made by possibly the most famous police force in the Empire made it an important decision likely to affect a number of forces from all over that Empire in their choice of weapon.

In March 1909, the board recommended that the Webley revolvers supplied to the force should be withdrawn and replaced by the Colt No.3 automatic pistol. Nothing happened until 1910 when the subject was raised again and the commissioner consulted the War Office on a suitable alternative weapon. On this occasion trials were conducted at the Army Inspection Department at Enfield Lock (not far from the scene of the robbery) by the Chief Inspector of Small Arms (the leading authority for the critical evaluation of military weapons). He suggested a British-made weapon, the Webley & Scott .32 calibre self-loading pistol be adopted with the same model in .22 calibre being adopted for training purposes. He also suggested that a number of officers from each division should receive training at Enfield so that they could act as instructors for the police service.

The Siege of Sidney Street on 3 January 1911 brought about the final recognition that the revolvers held by the MPS were too few in number and outdated and the search began immediately for a replacement. On 12 January 1911, 14 modern self-loading pistols were tried out at the small-bore rifle range of the 24th (County of London) Territorial Battalion at Kennington. Among those present were the Home Secretary, Winston Churchill, the MPS commissioner, Sir Edward Henry, and Robert Churchill a renowned gunsmith.

When the question whether they would like to start the tests was addressed to "Mr Churchill" there was some confusion. Winston the politician and Robert the gunsmith both reached for the first weapon, but the politician gave way to the gunsmith although the politician later fired several of the guns and showed great interest in the Mauser, a pistol which he had carried in the Sudan Campaign and again in the Second World War.

As a result it was thought that three different pistols would be required. One was to be for general uniform branch duty (to be carried in a holster) with a smaller one for CID officers (to be carried in a pocket) and finally one that would be used just for instructional purposes. With the assistance of the Chief Inspector of Small Arms at Enfield, Lieutenant-Colonel Tisdall, the MPS then drew up a 12-point specification for the new pistols. This included the requirement that they have sufficient stopping power, be accurate at up to 50 yards, have easily changeable magazines, must indicate when the last shot in the magazine had been fired and the larger pistol should have a lanyard attachment.

Pistols

Webley & Scott put forward its .38 Model 1910 (Type III) for the larger pistol and its .32 Model 1905 for the other, although modifications had to be made to both to meet the specification. For training, the company had a .22 calibre single-shot version which was not in production but used modified .32 calibre parts. During trials in April at Enfield the .38 fired during a drop test. Changes were made by the company and both .38 and the .32 passed all the tests the following month. Major de la Bere from

Enfield presented a report to Henry on the results and separate trials to determine stopping power were carried out using sheep carcasses in July.

Having studied all the reports Henry decided that the force would adopt just the .32 pistol for operational purposes (ammunition supply was simpler and it could be carried in a holster or in a pocket) with the single-shot .22 for training. The first order for 1,000 of these weapons was placed in October for what was to become known as the .32 calibre Webley & Scott "MP" model self-loading pistol together with 100 of the .22 training version.

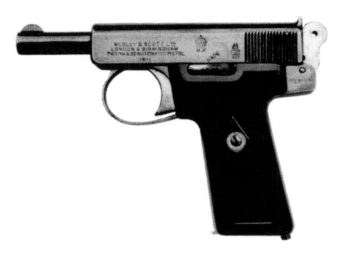

Webley & Scott 32 calibre "MP" model self-loading pistol

It is known that the "MP" model was subsequently adopted by forces in the City of London, Nottinghamshire, Oxfordshire, North Riding of Yorkshire, Norfolk, Sussex, Liverpool, Leicester and Hastings. There were undoubtedly others and to encourage marksmanship in the police a new annual shooting competition using the pistol was introduced at Bisley in 1925. It was open to teams of four from any police force and at the first meeting there were 20 teams competing for the Mander Challenge Cup (named after Captain John Harold Mander, the Chief Constable of Norfolk Constabulary). The "MP" would remain in use as the main MPS police handgun (other than for a period during World War Two) until it was replaced by the Webley & Scott .380 Mark IV revolver in 1956.

Since 1908, correspondence had passed between the Royal Navy and the MPS on the question of guarding HM ships refitted at Royal Dockyards. It had been suggested that the armed Royal Marine pickets should be replaced by constables (also armed). As police, especially the superintendent at Portsmouth Dockyard, refused to be held responsible for fittings and stores on board, or for the safety of the ship, the Admiralty finally shelved the idea in June 1911. This question of armed police in dockyards may have prompted a Police Order dated 3 November 1911.

"Police armed with revolvers are, when they detect the approach of any person or persons whose actions are suspicious, to challenge such person or persons by calling out, 'Halt, who goes there.' If the person or persons fail to reply to the challenge or to give a satisfactory explanation and continue to advance, the Constable should, if circumstances permit, repeat the challenge and warn them that unless they stop he will fire, at the same time, if possible, blowing his whistle. If they still advance, and he has reason to infer from their actions or from the surrounding circumstances, that they are evilly disposed, it will be necessary for him to fire with the object of disabling them

On hearing the sound of the police whistle, or the discharge of firearms, Police on adjoining beats are to hasten in the direction of the alarm and render assistance. A communication stating the cause of the disturbance and exact locality is to be sent as early as possible to the Officer in charge of the Establishment.

The officer in charge, on receipt of the alarm, will instantly call out all resident Police, and after issuing the available revolvers, direct them to proceed forthwith to the place indicated, where they will act as directed by the officer in charge.

It must be borne in mind that in any emergency the Superintendent should be informed at the earliest possible opportunity, in order that he may take over the direction of further police enquiries.

The foregoing instructions apply especially to Magazine Stations, but are to be observed in all cases where Police are especially armed for the purpose of protecting property."

Apart from introducing the standard challenge, which would have been a familiar warning to anyone in a naval or military station, the order states that the suspect should be "disabled." This word can be interpreted in several ways, even when facing the "evilly disposed" but it implies that the officer should fire to stop rather than to kill. Current police training is to aim at the largest available target, the person's chest and head, as his or her arms and legs can move out of the way unpredictably. It is quite difficult to find a way to put a bullet into a person's chest or head without killing him or her, however good a marksman you are. This point was brought home to me a few years ago. A man levelled a shotgun at me from behind a wall. If he fired he would have cut me in half. I was armed with a revolver, but could only see his head. I shot him in the head and killed him. When asked why I had fired I said that I had felt that my life was at risk from the shotgun aimed at me. When asked what I was attempting to do by shooting, I remembered my training and said that I wanted to stop the man killing me. I was later told that if I had said that I wanted to kill him then I would have been charged with murder. It is a legal technicality as it is impossible to shoot a man in the head and not expect to kill him.

During the last two months of 1911, a total of 920 Webley & Scott .32 pistols, complete with two magazines and 16 rounds for each weapon, were delivered and issued to divisions. Clearly this was insufficient. Would you enter a two hour gun battle with two men who held 400 rounds of ammunition between them when you had just 16? You don't get to quietly walk away when you run out of ammunition or luck. This isn't poker!

Another six pistols were provided for the Preparatory Class and a number of divisional officers were selected to be trained as instructors for the new weapon in Enfield. All .45 revolvers were returned to store for the receiver. In March 1912, the 100 .22 pistols were issued to stations for the use of Divisional Shooting Clubs which formed part of the MPS Shooting League. The league was made responsible for producing printed safety regulations and the commissioner, in a memorandum to his superintendents dated 25 June 1912, outlined the conditions of use for the training pistols. They were only to be used "under the guidance of officers who had been trained at Enfield or elsewhere" and a special grant of 10,000 rounds of .22 ammunition would be made "so as to afford as many as possible an opportunity of a preliminary practice." Obviously, the chance to allow men to practice in their own time with a weapon similar in weight and type to an operational pistol was too good to miss.

These weapons were not made available to dockyard police who later exchanged their naval Webley Mark IV revolvers for the .455 self-loading pistol when it was adopted by the Royal Navy in 1913.

Clearly, the weapons used by the robbers were vastly superior to those being used by the police In addition, the robbers held vastly superior stocks of ammunition and would be able to continue any gun battle far longer than the police could. Large numbers of the population held private weapons, which were not controlled at that time and which they had collected whilst serving in the services, or whilst travelling overseas and which would be an essential feature of this incident, particularly when the police were unable to access their own weapons for the locked gun cupboard in Tottenham Police Station.

Armed Robbery

Armed robberies require a great detail of planning. Gangs proposing to conduct one employ a man called a "draftsman" to design a plan that will include details of the person or company to be robbed, the strength of the defences that they will face in the robbery, the likely "take" in terms of the cash that they will accrue after the robbery, how many people will be required to conduct the robbery, the roles of each member of the gang, the value of a "share" for each member of the gang, the vehicles and the weapons that they will require and their escape route for the getaway.

Paul Helfeld had worked at the Rubber Company, so he knew what he was paid there and he knew that the company employed about 150 people, so he could work out the value of their weekly payroll. He also knew that he was working with Jacob Lepidus, so presumably they had agreed to take half each of whatever they stole. He knew the two people who always made the collection from the bank, the boy who was the wages clerk and the man who was the company chauffeur, they obviously felt that they could point their guns at them and get them to hand over the money, beat them in a fight if necessary and run off with the money without getting caught.

There are two competing versions of how the Latvians secured the weapons that they needed:

1. It has been claimed that they had been engaged in smuggling fire-arms and propaganda into Latvia for two years when they arrived in the United Kingdom and that they brought 50 of the latest semi-automatic and automatic weapons and several thousand rounds of ammunition with them, that they declared them to the customs officer at their point of entry and that he checked it all and waved it through. The law at the start of the 20th-century did not pre-vent or restrict the import, export, purchase, sale or possession of firearms, so this is entirely credible, as unlikely as it seems today.

2. At the time of the robbery, neither of the robbers owned a gun but Helfeld knew a man called Leon Beron who would rent them a couple of pistols in exchange for a share of the proceeds. Police knew Beron as a fence who worked out of Café Warsaw in Osborne Street in the East End. In the days after the Tottenham Outrage, the police looked closely at Beron and his activities. However, when Helfeld eventually died the enquiry very quickly closed down. Within two years, on New Year's Day 1911, Beron's battered body was discovered on Clapham Common and it set in motion the most notorious murder trial of the day with some of the East End's most colourful characters giving evidence.

More About Firearms ...

At the start of the 20th-century, the government saw Customs & Excise as an income generator. They were more interested in using it to collect cash than to restrict the importation and exportation of any controlled goods. The first prosecution for the illegal importation of firearms or ammunition did not take place until 1905 when one Heinrich Fischer tried to smuggle one million rounds of ammunition out of Newcastle to Russia by ship. Fischer was a German national and an associate of Lenin. He was arrested in St Petersburg in 1896 when it was the capital of Russia. He was sentenced to hard labour in an Artic labour camp and upon his release he was thrown out of Russia, did not fancy living in Germany, and moved to England, where he married and had two sons. He then started a business smuggling goods from Newcastle to Russia.

Between 1890 and 1910 firearms manufacturers across the world engaged in a race to produce the first automatic, and the first semi-automatic, pistols. After half a century of producing standard revolvers, the time had come for a new, ground-breaking design. Manufacturers across Western Europe and the USA were at the forefront of this research.

An automatic pistol would allow the user to continue to fire rounds as long as he or she continued to apply pressure to the trigger and as long as the weapon was still loaded with ammunition. A semi-automatic, or self-loading, pistol would require a separate trigger pull to fire each round, but would keep loading the rounds into the chamber faster than the user could pull the trigger. Before these weapons existed pistols would have to be cocked before each shot.

During the robbery in Tottenham, Paul Helfeld was armed with a Browning FNM1900 .32 calibre magazine-fed self-loading pistol.

Browning FN M1900

The Browning FN M1900 is a single-action, semi-automatic pistol designed in 1896 by John Browning. It was the first production hand-gun to use the slide, now a component of almost every modern-day pistol. Like many small gun designers of his era, Browning lacked the infrastructure and capital to manufacture the weapon in the required numbers and was compelled to licence its manufacture in Belgium by *Fabrique Nationale de Herstal* (FN). As a consequence the pistol came to be known by a number of other names including the FN M1900, the FN Mle.1900, the Browning M1900 and the Browning No.1; it is also closely linked to the Colt M1900, the FN Model 1903, and the FN 1900 pistol.

The M1900 was produced for eleven years, until 1910, by which time 700,000 existed. However, between 1927 and 1950 the Chinese copied it for use in the Second Sino-Japanese War and the Chinese Civil War and in 1964 the North Koreans also did so, adapted for use with a silencer, and called it the Type 64 pistol.

The M1900 was a popular gun used by many people. For example, Theodore Roosevelt, President of the USA (1901 to 1909) owned one with mother of pearl grips, which he regularly kept on his person or in his bedside drawer until the day he died. On 16 June 1904 Eugene Schauman, a Finnish nobleman and patriot, shot the Russian Governor-General of Finland, Nikolai Ivanovich Bobrikov three time with an M1900 as he came to the Senate House; he then shot himself twice in the chest. All the bullets that he used were hand-loaded explosive bullets. Schauman died instantly and Bobrikov the same night. On 26 October 1909, An Jung-Geun, Korean patriot, assassinated Itō Hirobumi, the four-times Japanese Prime Minister and former Resident-General of Korea, with an M1900 following the signing of the Eulsa Treaty, when it appeared likely that Japan would annex Korea. On 28 June 1914 Gavrilo Princip, a Bosnian-Serb patriot assassinated Archduke Franz Ferdinand of Austria in Sarajevo, in an incident that triggered the First World War. Contrary to numerous reports the gun that he used was an FN1910 and not an M1900.

During the robbery in Tottenham, Jakob Lepidus was armed with a Bergmann 1894 6.5mm magazine-fed self-loading pistol.

Bergmann 1894 6.5mm magazine-fed self-loading pistol.

Theodor Bergmann (21 May 1850 to 23 March 1931) was a German engineer and entrepreneur who ran a company that made pedal cycles. As an engineer, though, he yearned to expand into making the new automobiles and firearms that were spreading across the world at the time. As news of the latest inventions and developments reached him, he experimented with them and attempted to find the improvement that would thrust him to the forefront of the market in one of his chosen fields. Unfortunately, he lacked the infrastructure or capital to develop his inventions so that he was compelled to licence others to manufacture the firearms that he designed and eventually had to sell his automobile business to Carl Benz, who then joined up with Mercedes to form the iconic brand Mercedes Benz.

At the end of the 19th-century the firearms industry was exploring new materials and working on developing the first semi-automatic and fully-automatic pistols. The first automatic pistol was made in Saint-Étienne, France by the Clair brothers but it was not until 1892 that *Osterreichische Waffenfabrik Gesellaftsch* produced an automatic pistol in significant numbers. In 1901 Bergmann designed the MG15 Light Machine Gun as used until the Second World War. Theodor Bergmann's company still exists but as a plastics manufacturer.

Guns would be a vital part of The Outrage and the chase. The police and the public had vastly different firearms and other weapons, dictated by completely different circumstances. Now the robbery could commence!

CHAPTER 5

The Participants

The Perpetrators

The two perpetrators of The Outrage, both Jews born in Riga, Latvia, then under Russian control, are known today as Jacob Lepidus and Paul Helfeld, although there is nothing to confirm these identities, which are generally believed to be false. In *Chapter 1* it was explained that their friend and compatriot, George Gardstein used no less than 12 aliases and there is no reason to think that these two men did not have around the same number. In addition, in the days after The Outrage, Lepidus was known as "Jacob", "Yacob" and "Lapidus" and this has continued in some of the subsequent literature. In 1909, Paul Helfeld gave his age as 21 years and Jacob Lepidus gave his as 30 years.

The first record that can be found of these names is in Paris in 1907, two years before the incident in Tottenham. On 1 May 1907, Jacob Lepidus' brother, known as Leiser Lapidus, had been walking with an accomplice in the *Bois de Vincennes*, intending to assassinate the French president, when a bomb that he had been carrying in his pocket for the purpose exploded prematurely, killing him and seriously injuring his accomplice. As soon as he recovered from his injuries, the unnamed accomplice was sentenced to penal servitude for carrying bombs and at the time of The Outrage he was still in prison.

Paul Helfeld and Jacob Lepidus had been living in Paris with Leiser at the time of the explosion, but in anticipation of the police enquiries that would inevitably follow, they escaped to Scotland, where they lived discretely for about a year until their money ran out, when they headed south to London. Little is known about the two men at this time except that they were members of an organization called *Leesma* (The Flame), an anarchist body originating in Russia. They were also believed to have criminal records in their own country, Latvia.

Upon arriving in Tottenham (sometimes known as "Little Russia" at the time, due to the number of Russians living there) both Helfeld and Lepidus joined the local branch of the Lettish (i.e. Latvian) Socialists Revolutionary Party, which met on Monday evenings in Ferry Lane. Lepidus was also a member of the *Boskeviky* (Extremists) section of the Lettish Revolutionaries, though it was later believed that his membership of these organizations was merely to cover his criminal acts, mainly robbery.

Initially, Paul Helfeld rented a room over a tobacconist's shop in Ferry Lane known as "The Cigar Stores" from the man who owned it, a Mr Sowerman. At the subsequent inquest into the deaths of PC William Tyler and Ralph Joscelyne, Mr Sowerman would tell the court that, upon moving in, Helfeld had brought with him a sack which contained clothes and books in the Lithuanian language (which Mr Sowerman admitted that he could not understand). Helfeld had been quiet in his ways, and showed no sign of his real character. His actions were erratic and he frequently would not return home until the early hours of the morning. Helfeld only stayed at the tobacconist's shop for two weeks before moving to 51 High Cross Road, where he lived until his death.

On 16 December 1908, Helfeld took employment as a labourer on piecework at Schnurmann's Rubber Company. Like so many of his immigrant contemporaries he did not give Schnurmann's his real name and was therefore entered on the time sheet by his nickname of "Elephant." He worked at Schnurmann's over the Christmas period, but left on 29 December 1909, three-and-a-half weeks before the robbery, stating that the work there was "too hard."

At the resumed inquest into the deaths of PC Tyler and Ralph Joscelyne in February, Schnurmann's manager, Paul Casewitz, told the court that Helfeld had been employed on unskilled work in a department with other foreigners. When questioned, Casewitz explained that any enquiries the company made about Helfeld, or any of the other immigrants, were always unsuccessful and he admitted that the foreigners sometimes wrote their own character references, or sent in references from non-existent people.

Jacob Lepidus lived at Ashley Road, Tottenham from December 1907 to March 1908 but left when he could not pay the rent, due to being unemployed. He then moved to Station Road, Tottenham, where he stayed until his death. At some stage he had also lived briefly at the Commercial Home, Commercial Road in east London.

Police enquiries revealed that Lepidus had worked at Lebus' Timber Yard in Tottenham, but could not confirm the dates of this employment. When the police searched Jacob's room, they discovered large amounts of anarchist literature, as they had also done in Helfeld's room. In fact, they found so much that a car was needed to carry it away. Police enquiries indicate that both men earned money by taking anarchist literature printed in London to Riga, Libau and other Baltic ports, and that, in order to avoid snooping officials both here and in Russia, they hid the material in their luggage.

The Victims

PC 403 "N" William Frederick Tyler

Mrs Emily Tyler (née Burfield)

PC 403 "N" William Frederick Tyler was, with his colleague PC Charles I Newman, the first officer to respond to the gunfire at Schnurmann's Rubber Factory and give chase. At the time of the incident he was on reserve duty at Tottenham Police Station. Tyler was born on 22 May 1877 at 1 Hope Cottage, Childs Hill, near Finchley, the third child, and second son, of market gardener Alfred Tyler and his wife, Susan (née Henn). His early childhood was spent at 4 Rosebud Cottage, Temperance Cottages, The Mead, Childs Hill, close to Finchley Fire Station and the North Circular Road, and he was educated at the nearby All Saints' Church School, starting shortly before his third birthday. His mother died when he was young.

His father, Alfred Tyler, re-married and the family then moved the short distance to Granville Villa, Finchley Road. He died in 1900, some nine years prior to The Outrage, and was survived by his second wife and the children of both marriages. William's paternal grandfather, Henry Tyler, had been a mushroom spawn maker, whose trade was worldwide. On leaving school, William joined his father in the business before going into the Army and becoming a gunner in the Royal Garrison Artillery, serving most of his six years in Gibraltar under Sir George White. At the time that William joined the Army he was under age. After his father's death Alfred inherited the family mushroom farm but then sold it.

After leaving the Army in 1903, William Tyler joined the MPS and was initially stationed at Stoke Newington. By 1909 he had completed six years' police service. He had an exemplary record and shortly before he left there had been commended both by the justices at Tottenham Petty Sessions and by the trial judge and grand jury at the Middlesex Sessions in connection with an incident that had taken place in 1908, in which he had saved the life of a woman attempting suicide. He was highly regarded by his superiors and was being strongly encouraged to apply for promotion to sergeant. On 29 January 1909, six days after The Outrage the *Hendon and Finchley Times* reported that Tyler was known to be very adaptable and was "particularly active in telegraphic operations."

PC Tyler's widow, Emily Tyler (née Burfield) was born on 8 February 1882 at 79 Brady Street, Bethnal Green, a house of multiple occupancy. She was the second daughter of William Burfield, a coal collector, and his wife Charlotte (née Klingsick) who was employed as a tailoress. Nothing is known of Emily's early years or where and when she met William, but they married in a civil ceremony at Holborn Registry Office on 28 July 1903, just after William had joined the MPS. Indeed, on their marriage certificate William's occupation was given as policeman and Emily was shown as being a sewing machinist.

Six years after The Outrage, Emily re-married, again to a policeman. On 15 April 1915 at St James the Less Church in Bethnal Green, she married PC William George Williams of "J" Division in Walthamstow He retired from the police in 1924 and opened a refreshment kiosk at Nevendon, on the new Southend arterial road. On 11 July 1925, he committed suicide, probably due to the failure of the business. The *Southend Standard* of 16 July 1925 carried the story, under the headline "Tragic Death at Crays Hill," The newspaper reported that Emily had found his body at their home at Oak Cottage, Crays Hill, Essex. On 6 February 1937, Emily died at Rochford Hospital, near Southend, Essex, just two days before her 55th birthday. The address given on her death certificate is that of the Nevendon Café, Nevendon, Essex.

The burial records for Abney Park Cemetery show that Emily shares the grave of her first husband, William Tyler, being interred there on 11 February 1937. In recent years, the Tyler grave was vandalised. The policeman's helmet and cape was knocked off the marble monument. Fortunately, it has now been restored to its former glory.

Ralph John Joscelyne is sometimes overlooked. He had just celebrated his tenth birthday in December; he was a pupil of nearby Earlsmead Infant and Junior School in Broad Lane, Tottenham, just 0.7 miles (1.1 kilometre) or a 15 minute walk from scene of his death. As usual on a Saturday, he had been helping the local baker with his rounds. Before leaving his home in Colsterworth Road that fateful morning he had wangled a farthing from his father, after first unsuccessfully trying for a halfpenny (At decimalisation in 1971, 2.4 old pennies became one new penny; a farthing was a quarter of an old penny, so that a farthing was worth just 0.1 of a new penny, or in other words, almost nothing today, but in those days it would have been enough to let young Ralph buy a home-made bun or soft drink from the market on his way home.)

As a ten-year-old, Ralph would not have carried a wallet and in the chaos he must have become separated from the baker for whom he was working, so the police and those who saw him shot down would not have known who he was or how they could inform his parents. Accordingly, it was not until the evening, when he had not arrived home, that his anxious parents called the police and were eventually informed of his death.

The Arresting Officers

After the perpetrators and victims, the most significant participants in The Outrage were the three police officers who finally resolved the situation. They entered Oak Cottage and went up the narrow staircase to the bedroom where Lepidus had taken refuge, in order to deal with him, either by arresting him, or if necessary to shoot and even kill him. The order in which they went up the stairs was PC 636 "J" Charles Eagles, DC Charles Dixon and PC 741 "N" John William Cater. The MPS records of the three officers confirm the following facts:

Charles Eagles (Warrant Number 68090) joined on 23 November 1903 and retired on 26 November 1928 as police sergeant 125 "P" at Peckham Police Station, having completed 25 years' service. His identity was confirmed by his promotion and his award of the King's Police Medal following the incident in 1909. Interestingly, at the time of that incident PC Eagles had five years two months service and if the incident had occurred eight weeks earlier, he would, like PC Ziething and PC Newman not have been eligible for promotion as he would not have had the five years' police service required by the regulations. His service record shows his shoulder number as PC 642 "N" and not PC 636 "N" as in Superintendent Jenkins' report.

Charles Dixon (No Warrant Number shown) joined on 28 May 1883 and retired on 1 April 1912 as a detective inspector, having completed 29 years ten months police service. At the time of the incident, in January 1909, he had already completed his 25 years' service that he required for a full pension and reached the time at which most officers would have retired.

John William Cater (Warrant Number 87890) joined on 14 October 1901 and retired on 18 October 1926 as station sergeant (SPS) 12 "Y". At the time of the incident he had seven years and three months service.

Interestingly, nothing else survives of PC Eagles. No researcher has ever reported hearing of him again after The Outrage. His photograph does not appear on the poster that was produced to commemorate The Outrage events and he just disappears from sight. It may be that as he comes from "J" Division there is some resentment that he should in some way become the star of the show and gain all the credit. Or, as historians say, "History is written by the victors" and this was a story written by Superintendent Jenkins and the senior officers at Tottenham and they may have focused on their own officers and their roles, rather than deflecting the praise onto an outsider, however grateful they were at the time for PC Eagles' assistance.

Indeed, there is little known about DC Dixon. The reasons for this may be similar to those in the case of PC Eagles. DC Dixon belonged to a small and select band of CID officers based at Tottenham Police Station. They may have considered themselves to be an elite unit so that the uniformed superintendent would have considered them to be under their own senior CID officers, rather under his command and he may therefore have focussed his praise on his own subordinates, so that it reflected well on him.

Fortunately, a little more is known about PC Cater. PC 741 "N" John William Cater was born on 8 January, 1880, in Soham, Cambridgeshire. In his early life, he worked as a groom in Cambridgeshire, and then moved to London and worked in service. His original aim had been to enlist in the Army, but he had been turned down due to having a hammer toe. Instead, he went on to join the MPS on 14 October 1901 when aged 21. At the time of The Tottenham Outrage, Cater, then 29, had been living in the police house next to Tottenham Police Station on the corner of Chesnut Avenue, where the infamous chase started. John was off duty at the time of the incident and in photographs of it he may be seen wearing a Guernsey jumper.

His son says John rarely mentioned the incident in his later years. He only recalled things that his father said when reading subsequent reports of the event that were made in the press from time-to-time. The one fact of which he is certain is that his father went back into Tottenham Police Station to obtain a firearm. He stayed with the chase for its entire duration, ending up with PCs Eagles and Dixon at Oak Cottage, where he and PC Dixon looked at one another, and decided that, *"You only die once...!"*. With that, the officers broke down the bedroom door and everybody fired at once. PC Eagles shot twice, PC Dixon shot once and Lepidus shot once and fell, dead, onto the bed. His son remembers that John had a photo of the bed on which Lepidus died, and of his firearm, but he cannot remember seeing it again after the family moved away from Finsbury Park.

After The Outrage, John remained at Tottenham Police Station and was promoted to sergeant without an exam. He was awarded the King's Police Medal, which had been created by the late Edward VII, following The Outrage, from HM King George V himself. He also received the Carnegie Medal for Gallantry in the Course of Duty (sometimes referred to as the Carnegie Medallion). Later in his service he was awarded two Coronation Medals, when he was assigned to duty on the Coronation Procession.

He married his wife, Hilda, when he was 35, when he was living in Holloway. His first son was born in 1916, by which time the family had moved to Coleridge Road, Finsbury Park. In 1918, John had a second son, who joined the RAF Volunteer Reserve, but he was killed when his plane came down in the Mediterranean.

The Injured Officers

PC Nicod on his promo-
tion in 1909

PC Nicod on his retire-
ment in 1924

PC William Henry Nicod was born in St Pancras, between Euston
and Kings Cross in north London. He joined the Army as soon as it
was permitted for him to do so and the Middlesex Regiment for eight
years. On leaving the Army he joined the MPS on 8 May 1899. Just a
few months later he was recalled to the Army for the South African War
and returned to his former regiment for its duration.

At The Outrage PC Nicod gave chase after the suspects until he stepped
ahead of it and knelt down in order to take careful aim at the perpetrators, when he was repeatedly shot and severely wounded. For his devotion
to duty and great courage he was specially promoted from constable to
sergeant, without having to pass the promotion examination. His gallant action also secured other recognition when he was subsequently
awarded the Carnegie Medal, the presentation being made by the then
Lord Mayor of London. The medal contains on one side the inscription,
"Presented to PC William Henry Nicod for heroic endeavour to save

human life" and on the reverse, "He serves God best who most nobly serves humanity."

During his police service, PC Nicod served at "N" Division (Edmonton), "S" Division (Albany Street) and "K" Division (Dagenham), where for 15 years he was the coroner's officer. He eventually retired in 1924, having completed 25 years' service, Nicod's father sent the following account from the *Weekly Herald,* Tottenham on 21 August 1908, six months before The Outrage, to his brother Alfred:

"William Barber (20), labourer of Railway Terrace, White Hart Lane, Tottenham, was charged with assaulting PC 313 "N" Nicod. W Chamberlain for the Commissioner of Police said that a number of charges could be preferred against the prisoner, but he asked the Bench to deal with him only on the present accusation. PC Nicod said that on 3 July the prisoner had been behaving in a disorderly manner in White Hart Lane, and as a caution had not been regarded, the witness apprehended him. The prisoner escaped, then threw him to the ground, and while he was down, kicked him in the face and elsewhere. A hostile crowd collected and the prisoner got away again, and ran into a private house, the door of which was locked against the witness. As a consequence he avoided apprehension. A warrant was obtained and the prisoner was apprehended at a later date. The injuries to the constable were not serious. It was proved that the prisoner had been previously convicted for assaulting the police and a publican. He was sentenced to six months hard labour."

CHAPTER 6

The Robbery

On 1 May 1907 an anarchist plot to kill the President of France in Paris had been aborted when the assassin's bomb exploded in his pocket and blew him to pieces. His surviving companions quickly crossed the English Channel and took false names. Two of them, now known as Paul Helfeld, aged 21, and Jacob Lepidus, the 35-year-old brother of the dead man, fled to Scotland and went into hiding for around a year. Eventually, desperately short of money, they made their way to London where Helfeld went to work at the Schnurmann's Rubber Factory in Tottenham, but left after a few days, complaining that the job was too hard, but not before he had studied the company's arrangements for paying its staff.

The Largest Rubber Buyers in the World.
J. SCHNURMANN
Downham Mills, 3–5 Chesnut Road, TOTTENHAM, LONDON, N.
We buy OLD WASTE INDIA-RUBBER of any kind
Please ask for our price list
Telegrams:— "RECLAIMING, LONDON"
Telephone:— "No. 93 TOTTENHAM"

Saturday 23 January 1909 was a very cold day. The breath of both animals and humans clouded in the icy air as they went about their business on that morning. A strong wind turned all the weather vanes to the north-east, tore smoke from chimneys, and caused heavy grey clouds to scud across the dull, gloomy sky while creaking shop signs appeared in danger of being ripped from their moorings. Buffeted pedestrians either fought against the bone-chilling wind or tried to stop themselves from being blown along before it. Passengers in motor cars were well wrapped up, while those travelling in trams and buses huddled together on the enclosed lower cabin, leaving the open, empty upper deck to the elements. Late January in 1909 had been typified by icy weather. As the *Daily Mirror* of 24 January 1909 reported, seven to ten degrees of frost had been registered the previous day, the day of the robbery and the thermometer had not risen above freezing point since. The newspaper predicted a continuation of this and stated that dry, cold conditions prevailed throughout the south-east of England.

Saturday was market day in Tottenham and at 9.30 a.m. the streets came to life as everybody prepared for a hard day's work. Market traders started putting up their stalls, setting out their wares and hoping for large crowds. In Tottenham Police Station the young officers posted to police the market were being woken and dragged from their beds to get ready for work. Outside the police station, in Chesnut Road, the two Latvians, Jacob Lepidus and Paul Helfeld arrived to do a job that they had planned for the day.

Inside the Police Station

In 1909, Tottenham Police Station stood on the same site that it currently occupies, at the junction of Tottenham High Road and Chesnut Road, but at that time the impressive 100 metre long, three storey frontage that now exists in Tottenham High Road had not yet been built and the main entrance to the police station was at the side of the building in Chesnut Road. In those days the upper floors of the building acted as a section house or barracks for unmarried officers, most of whom had been posted to police the market that day.

As they got out of bed and pulled themselves together, all the young police officers were looking to have a shave, a shower, to clean their teeth and to use the toilet. Then it would be time to have something to eat and drink and get dressed. Those who had taken a drink the night before and those who had stayed up late talking to friends would have found all this stressful. Thirty sleepy guys in a confined space, all trying to do the same things at the same time, bumping into each other.

If still tired and grumpy, possibly with a hangover, then they might all snap at each other.

At that time there were no modern fabrics and uniforms were made from wool and cotton. They were high maintenance and the facilities for washing, drying and ironing them were severely limited in police stations. There was a large Belfast sink in the basement for washing clothes and each officer had to have his own bar of soap to do the washing, as there were no washing powders in those days, it was just good, old fashioned elbow grease. The room next to the boiler in the basement was too hot for anything else, so it had been set aside as a drying room, where officers who had performed duty in rain, sleet or snow, could put their clothes, so that they could dry off before it was time to put them back on again 16 or maybe just eight hours later. At this time an iron was a heavy lump of metal that could be placed on the boiler to warm up so that it could be used to press items of clothing until it cooled down again.

In those days policemen spent their time on duty walking constantly up and down the same streets, irrespective of the weather. Many of them had served in the armed forces, where they had learned the benefit of wearing a good, strong pair of leather boots and of taking great care of them. "Take care of your boots and they will take care of you." It is impossible to polish wet books, so the first priority at the end of the shift would always be to slowly dry them so that they did not split, then, at the last possible minute, to polish them so that they shone, as required by senior officers.

Punctuality and a smart appearance were the two priorities in those days. Sergeants who had served in the armed services would be strict when checking the appearance of their officers. Every duty would commence with a parade when police officers would be expected to attend 15 minutes before their duty began, to be inspected for their appearance, to present their truncheons, whistles and pocket books, to receive their postings and instructions and be sent out to work.

With officers getting only one Sunday off every second week there was little time to prepare the uniform, especially after rain, sleet or snow when thick woollen greatcoats had been soaked through and needed to be placed in the drying room in the basement. Instead of the modern, drip-dry, white shirts of today, the officers were supplied with three blue cotton shirts that took days to dry and hours to iron, so that officers wore them for two or three days before washing them. Fortunately, the old blue shirts came with detachable collars and cuffs, so that these could be washed separately whilst still wearing the body of the shirt. Unfortunately, it was hard to attach these to the shirt, with metal studs at the back and front of the collar.

By 10 a.m. all the police constables in Tottenham would have been struggling with their uniforms and preparing for duty. Collecting greatcoats, tunics and trousers from the drying room and negotiating to use an iron and ironing board to press them for work. Wrestling with boots that were probably still damp to get them on their feet. Twisting and stretching to fit the metal studs into the shirts and attach the collars and cuffs.

On the Streets Outside... and Schnurmann's Payroll

Also at about 9.30 a.m., the two Latvians prepared for work. These men, later described by witnesses as being "of foreign appearance", were seen loitering outside the premises of Frederick William Perry, a photographer, at 6 Chesnut Road, Tottenham, just two doors away from Tottenham Police Station. Lepidus, tall, dark-skinned with a drooping black moustache and Helfeld, shorter, fairer and clean-shaven, were seen to walk up and down and look in shop windows. A few local people, suspicious about their behaviour, approached the two men and asked them if they were all right or whether they needed anything, but they declined any offers of assistance and said that they were simply waiting for friends.

The two men did not appear interested in Mr Perry's shop display but kept glancing across the road at the Schnurmann factory opposite, using the shop window as a mirror to observe it in-between times. The Schnurmann Rubber Factory was situated at 3 to 5 Chesnut Road, Tottenham. The company salvaged and re-cycled used rubber from second-hand cars and described itself as "The Largest Rubber Buyers in the World."

At the start of the 20th-century, rubber was Tottenham's biggest and most important industry. The plentiful cheap housing combined with easy access to the London Docks for the importation of the rubber and the exportation of manufactured goods was ideal. There were two rubber factories in Tottenham at the time, the India Rubber Company and the Schnurmann Rubber Company. Schnurmann was a highly successful global business with its own rubber plantations in the Dutch East Indies and factories in the United Kingdom and USA. Schnurmann relied on paying lower wages and undercutting its rival's prices for its success. The wages were so low that no British people would work for the company and in 1902 there had been rioting at the factory in Chesnut Road about this. Eventually only immigrants would work for the company and it was prepared to accept false particulars, nicknames and even random numbers from potential employees in order to secure staff. Schnurmann's employed about 150 people with a total weekly wage bill of just £80, equivalent today to £8,640 after inflation, an average of around 50p (or ten shillings) per employee per week. Eventually the two men crossed the road, meandering along the pavement and chatting together before positioning themselves on either side of Schnurmann's gates, Helfeld to the right and Lepidus to the left.

Inside the factory office, unaware of the two men loitering outside his gates, the proprietor Julius Schnurmann stood at the window, gazing out anxiously in the direction of Tottenham High Road. He was looking for his motor car containing his chauffeur, Joseph Wilson, and his office boy, Albert Keyworth, who were due to return from their regular weekly visit to the London and South Western Bank in Hackney, where they collected the weekly payroll. Leaving the factory on an errand, 16-year-old Charles Allison had nodded a greeting to Helfeld, whom he recognised as "Elephant," who had briefly worked at the factory, three-and-a-half weeks earlier.

In the early 20th-century, working practices were considerably different to what they are today. Men went out to work to financially support their family and expected long, harsh days of vigorous hard work. Women invariably stayed at home and without the white goods and cleaning materials that exist today used hard work to clean their homes; they looked after their family and were expected to have the man's tea on the table when he got home from work. Few homes had electricity in those days, so they were lit by gas and there were no televisions, computers, sound systems or such like. So, exhausted after their exertions, people went to bed around nine or ten o'clock.

Factory owners asserted their authority at every opportunity and the vast majority liked to pay their workers cash-in-hand, just to let them know who was in charge. This also suited the workers, few if any of whom would have had their own bank accounts at the time. At the start of the 20th-century wages were low and for most of the workers it would have been a hand-to-mouth existence, with men having to borrow money to feed their families before and until pay day, re-paying those loans when they received their wages and then spending any remaining cash on intoxicating liquor, so that they had to borrow yet more money to feed the family.

Of course, paying cash-in-hand meant moving substantial sums of money around on Fridays and Saturdays when the wages fell due. There were no security vans in those days as they only appeared after the boom in armed robbery in the 1970s and 1980s. Cash would have to be collected from the bank and delivered to the factory, usually by two old ladies or two young boys, or a combination of the two, not exactly the most secure system in the world. At the factory somebody had to work out exactly how much each person was entitled to in pay, allowances and expenses and just how much income tax they had to pay, and put exactly the right amount of money in each person's pay packet, or there would be trouble!

At the same time every Saturday morning Julius Schnurmann dispatched the same chauffeur, Joseph Wilson (aged 39), and the same wages clerk, Albert Keyworth (aged 17) to the same London and South Western Bank in South Hackney in the same company car; every time they drove along the same route carrying the same bag. Every week the men collected the same £80 in gold, silver and copper coin, weighing 21 pounds, to pay the workers. In those days nobody earned enough money to be paid in banknotes and certainly not at low-paying Schnurmann's.

It is only natural that when the same people do the same thing on the same day and at the same time over and over again, they tend to develop a monotonous routine and Paul Helfeld quickly recognised this and discussed it with his friend, Jacob Lepidus, and they formed a plan to rob the wages for themselves.

The Robbery

George Smith, a stoker at Hornsey Gasworks, was out for his morning constitutional. Having told his family he needed to blow away the cobwebs before going to work he had left his home at nearby Scotland Green and walked along the High Road. He entered Chesnut Road as Charles Allison returned from his errand and the car arrived, slowing down to allow Albert Keyworth to alight. Further down Chesnut Road, outside number 15, Mrs Mary Cawley wrapped her shawl tighter against the icy wind as she chatted with the greengrocer while selecting her vegetables from his cart. She noticed the motor car pull up.

As it drew up outside the factory, Keyworth got out and crossed the pavement carrying the bag containing the company wages. As he passed through the factory gates, he was grabbed from behind by Jacob Lepidus, who attempted to snatch the bag from him. The two men fell to the ground and rolled around into the middle of the road, where with Lepidus still on top of him, Keyworth called on Wilson to help him. Lepidus then put his hands around Keyworth's throat and attempted the throttle him in an attempt to loosen his grip on the bag.

It was at this point that James Wilson got out of the car, ran over to where the two men were fighting and put a headlock on Lepidus and pulled him off Keyworth. Seeing this, Helfeld ran up to Wilson, produced his pistol, a Browning FNM1900 .32 calibre magazine-fed self-loading weapon, took aim, and fired several shots at him. Due to the cold weather, Wilson was wearing several layers of clothing, topped off with a heavy ankle-length driving coat and it was later found that his coat was riddled with bullet holes and that one slanting shot across the front of his body had penetrated his coat, jacket, shirt and even his vest, but not his body. In the words of Superintendent Jenkins' subsequent police report: "in a *miraculous and unaccountable way, he escaped injury*" (emphasis added). Clearly, the thickness of his coat saved Wilson's life.

By now Lepidus had finally managed to get the wages bag off Keyworth. As the two men recovered their feet and faced each other, Lepidus drew his pistol, Lepidus produced a Bergmann 1894 6.5 mm magazine-fed self-loading pistol, and aimed it at Keyworth, but missed. Hearing the commotion and Keyworth's pleas for assistance, George Smith hid behind a parked and unattended motor vehicle outside the factory in Chesnut Road. As Lepidus started to run out of the factory with the wages bag, Smith jumped from his hiding place and made a flying rugby-style tackle on him, taking him to the ground. Helfeld then emerged from where he had been waiting behind the factory gates and ran over to straddle the two men as they fought on the ground. He then aimed his pistol at Smith's head and fired four times. Two bullets creased Smith's scalp, one missed and the other hit him in the chest below the collarbone. His *"escape from death was equally remarkable"* (emphasis added) stated Superintendent Jenkins in his report, and Smith survived to be photographed proudly wearing his bullet-holed coat.

Shaken and stunned by the bullets, Smith released his grip on Lepidus who ran off down Chesnut Road, hiding the wages bag inside his jacket, the last time that it was ever seen. Helfeld ran after Lepidus and joined him in taking pot shots at their pursuers as they ran down Chesnut Road.

The two Latvians were armed with two of the latest and most advanced handguns in the world at that time and, although nobody realised it as they robbed Keyworth, the robbers had brought four hundred rounds of ammunition with them. In fact, this was very likely equal to more than ten per cent of the total quantity of ammunition that the MPS owned across the whole of London at that time; police in London were usually only issued with ten rounds when given a revolver. The other indeterminate factor at this time was just how well-trained Helfeld and Lepidus were with their state-of-the-art weapons. It is unclear whether they had ever served in the Russian Army, or whether, as anarchists they had undergone any sort of weapons training. Having spent considerable sums to purchase the latest weapons and ammunition and being dedicated to the armed overthrow of government, it should be assumed that they would have undergone some sort of weapons training.

All these issues eventually proved to be irrelevant. It had been so long since firearms had been issued in Tottenham that when the gunshots were heard, and consideration was eventually given for weapons to be issued to police officers, the key for the gun cupboard could not be found. Extensive efforts were made to locate the keys and eventually cutlasses were issued instead, quite possibly the last occasion when officers were issued with swords in London.

As first shots rang out everybody stopped what they were doing and ran out into Chesnut Road to do what needed to be done. There wouldn't be a parade today! So it was that 30-odd policemen ran into Chesnut Road half-dressed and half-undressed. Officers who were usually only permitted to go onto the streets after they had been formally inspected by their senior officers and who were therefore always extremely smart and paragons of their community ran out with or without their trousers, with or without their boots, trying to fit their collars to their shirts and to put on their ties and helmets. Several officers subsequently made claims for compensation for uniform that dropped off during the chase and which, according to regulations they were required to pay for, and for colds, influenza and chills that they picked up whilst chasing the Latvians through the streets.

George Smith struggled to get to his feet to chase after the two robbers, but it was at this moment that the first police officers arrived on the scene. Responding to the shots that they had heard and having seen Smith fighting with Lepidus, and unsure of what had happened, they grabbed hold of Smith and took him back to the police station for questioning. More police officers then arrived at the scene. PC Newman persuaded James Wilson to get back in the car and to drive down Chesnut Road after the two robbers. PC Tyler ran after them. They were followed by several night duty officers who, awoken by the commotion, hastily donned clothing and ran out of the front entrance.

By now Helfeld and Lepidus had run past Mrs Cawley who, having seen the robbers fire shots at Keyworth and Smith and the two victims fall down, screamed "Murder! Stop those two men!" as she grabbed a potato from a greengrocer's cart and lobbed it at the gunmen. One of robbers stopped, pointed his gun at her but then decided not to fire.

PC Frasier, who had been in the boot room and PC Bond, who had been shaving in the bathroom when the firing broke out, ran down the stairs, grabbed a truncheon each, and without stopping to put on a shirt or tunic, jumped through the open window of the station's ground floor locker-room and joined the chase. Most of the constables were on foot, but some commandeered bicycles and pedalled furiously in pursuit. Those waving cutlasses above their head as they pursued the robbers looked particularly ridiculous as they struggled to control their machines. Hearing the commotion, off duty policemen began running from Tottenham Police Station. Some had been asleep in the section house and grabbed their clothes before hurrying out. Others did not bother to dress fully, but went as they were, scrambling through the front door of the station.

The chase was now on ...

CHAPTER 7

The Hue and Cry

Most people enjoy a good cop show and a key element of these is the police chase. Although not quite a cop, James Bond is a government agent chasing bad guys and today no Bond film would be complete without our hero jumping from jets to helicopters to speedboats to the latest supercars and back again. Nobody who has seen Steve McQueen in the 1968 film *Bullitt*, widely-acclaimed as featuring the finest police chase in film history, through the streets of San Francisco, will ever forget it. All that excitement in a simple American muscle car, a red Ford Mustang! The fact that the participants in our own story used horses and carts, milk floats and old-fashioned trams, and not McLarens or Aston Martins, matters not at all. The fact that the policemen at least started the chase waving wooden truncheons and waving cutlasses above their heads instead of carrying Heckler and Kock MP5s or Mac 10s does not diminish the chase at all.

The Nature of the Chase

Ultimately, it is not the size and power of the vehicles involved, or the calibre of the weapons, that makes a good chase. It is the fact that two individuals or two teams are in a life and death pursuit; observing their good fortune and their bad luck, experiencing the drama as situations arise, and are resolved, as first one and then the other takes the lead, to make sure that good or evil will prevail, etc. etc. This was all about the outcome. Whether the robbers would get away or whether they would die attempting to do so. It is the drama of the chase that really grabs our attention and makes our hearts race. Will they catch the bad guy or not?

The hue and cry that followed the robbery at Tottenham consisted of two young robbers on foot pursued by around 1,000 members of the general public, most of whom were also on foot, but some of whom were on horseback, on pedal cycles, or in horse drawn carts. After a minute or two, policemen started joining the chase, in response to hearing the shots fired by the robbers. Some of the officers were on reserve duty in the police station, some lived in the police section house accommodation above it, and some in the married quarters next to the police station, at the junction with Tottenham High Road. They would have been taught to find out as much as they could about suspects before they confronted them and they would have been a little cautious and keen to find out what had happened, and how the suspects were armed, before joining the chase and putting themselves in danger.

As the chase continued officers from the surrounding police stations joined in, until witnesses refer to there being around 100 officers in total involved towards the end. Of course, as the number of police officers increased, it is also likely that the number of private citizens involved diminished, as people became tired or started to realise the danger that they faced, or simply went home to collect firearms and could not find the chase again, or were unable to circumnavigate the railway bridges, rivers, reservoirs and streams that the route crossed.

Throughout the chase, the robbers maintained a fast walking pace of three miles per hour from start to finish; but they were not always walking. They sprinted when confronted by armed officers or members of the public; they stopped for several minutes when facing off their pursuers and attempting to deter them from continuing by taking carefully aimed shots at them, then they sprinted again. They ran through marshland and climbed over walls and fences. All this was quite tiring and speaks well of the Latvians' fitness, although by the end they were totally exhausted.

Of course, the robbers were still armed from the robbery and throughout the chase they fired a shot on average every 22 seconds. Most policemen facing desperate armed men want a firearm themselves and so it was that messages came to be sent to Tottenham Police Station for guns to be issued and sent to the scene. Unfortunately, none were forthcoming although a number of cutlasses were issued to police officers, which although they would have emboldened the officers, would have been little use against the latest, state of the art, European semi-automatic pistols.

But this was not just the police chasing two dangerous criminals down the road; it was the community responding to an outrage. Young men, old men, young women and old women all chased the two robbers through the streets and across The Marshes, taking pot shots at them. Men on crutches and women in wheelchairs all joined the pursuit. Many of these citizens were armed to the teeth with their own revolvers, pistols, rifles and shotguns, collected whilst serving in the British Army in some far off conflict or during a holiday abroad. And they were not afraid to use their weapons to defend themselves or to assist their police to apprehend the robbers.

The policemen, usually restrained, calm, upright bastions of the law walking slowly down the road in carefully pressed uniforms and polished boots, ran down the road only half dressed, or even wearing pyjamas, with others covered in soap, without shirts, boots and helmets, riding pedal cycles whilst waving cutlasses over their heads. The sight of these pillars of the Establishment running around in this state makes it hilarious and several correspondents referred to the Keystone Cops, the heroes of the silent movies of the time, in their reports.

English common law established the principal of hue and cry in medieval times; It was subsequently incorporated into law by the Statute of Winchester in the year 1285 (13 Edw. I cc. 1 and 4). Having existed for so long it has passed the test of time and is currently incorporated into the law of many USA states.

Hue and cry requires that all able-bodied men (or women), whether a police constable or a private citizen, are summoned to assist in the apprehension of a criminal who has been witnessed in the act of committing a crime and that the hue and cry must be kept up against the fleeing criminal from place-to-place, town-to-town and county-to-county, until the felon is apprehended and delivered to the authorities, originally to the sheriff.

The law never made it a criminal offence to fail to participate in a hue and cry, although a person who falsely raised one was considered to be guilty of a crime. Instead, the law made all the other local adult male residents equally responsible for the crime if they failed to participate and liable to be punished for their failure.

At the start of the 20th-century when houses and flats were shared by several families due to their cost, and where money was extremely tight and people frequently had to lend and borrow it to feed their families and where poor housekeeping could lead to a plague, there was a strong sense of community and people would have been more prepared to get involved in detaining an offender than they are today when people tend to wave their pay slips and point out that they have contributed substantial amounts in income tax to provide a police service to do the job for them.

Imagine how Helfeld and Lepidus must have felt as they ran away from the rubber factory. Both had fired their weapons at the pay clerks who, like most men, fell down when shot at, even when they have not been hit. They see the flash and the explosion and assume that they have been hit until they have had an opportunity to pat themselves down, make sure that everything works, and confirm that the bullets missed. The Latvians would have run off at speed suspecting that they had struck their targets and probably believing that they were dead or dying and that they now faced the death penalty if they were apprehended.

Everywhere the Latvians looked there were people coming towards them. What should they do? Which way should they go? Who else was armed, either with a gun or a sword or a stick? As already described, the two men fired a shot on average every 20 seconds for the entire duration of the chase. Clearly, they hoped that this would remind their pursuers of the threat that they posed. Just how many of these shots were carefully aimed and how many were simply shots in the air is not clear. If you think that the whole world is against you and that you face the death penalty if captured it would no doubt be extremely stressful.

The formation of the Metropolitan Police Service (MPS or "The Met": originally as a "force" but nowadays as a "service", the term used for convenience throughout this book) in 1829 did little to change the principle of hue and cry and the police still relied heavily on the support of the public in detaining offenders. The value of hue and cry was acknowledged by the MPS when they employed the term as the original title of the journal that they used to circulate the names and personal details of people that they sought to arrest, before it was renamed as the *Police Gazette*. However, the introduction in the 1920s of wireless (R/T) cars, fast pursuit vehicles driven by highly-trained police officers trained at the MPS Driving School in Hendon, and controlled via VHF radio meant that they were then able to detain offenders without the same need for public assistance.

The MPS has more police officers and more civilian staff than all the other police services in England and Wales put together. Covering the area of Greater London inside the M25 motorway, it is currently fast approaching its second centenary. The pursuit of Helfeld and Lepidus is the longest, most violent, most dramatic, most exciting police chase in the history of the MPS and quite possibly that of the entire British Police Service.

Helfeld and Lepidus Try to Make their Getaway...

As Helfeld and Lepidus took off down Chesnut Road, armed with two of the most modern and lethal handguns in the world and 400 rounds of high-power ammunition, they can have had little imagination of what lay ahead of them. Having only recently moved to England, they would not have known the area well and it is unlikely that their planning for the robbery had included a recce of the area and potential getaway routes. Each turn potentially led to a cul-de-sac, where they could be trapped by their pursuers.

The pair ran from the scene of their crime down Chesnut Road. As PC Newman left the police station he was accosted by one of the victims of the crime, company chauffeur, Joseph Wilson, who told him what had happened. Newman told Wilson to get back in the car and crouched on the running board himself, Mr Schnurmann got into the front passenger seat whilst Paul Casewitz, Schnurmann's manager, and young Albert Keyworth, the second victim of the robbery, jumped in the back seat. PC Tyler ran alongside the car, holding onto the left-hand (passenger side) door. Wilson, now recovered from the robbery itself, started the car and honked the horn to clear a pathway through the rapidly gathering crowd, in an attempt to catch up with the two gunmen, who were, by now, in Mitchley Road.

Many men were now joining the chase. Among these were Sub-Divisional Police Inspector Large, who had his horse saddled-up, Charles Allison from the Schnurmann factory and Frederick Perry (aged 17), the son of the owner of the photographic shop, who had rushed from there in his shirtsleeves, PCs Bond and Frasier who had jumped out of the locker room window and many more police officers, who had heard the shots fired during the robbery, and who had been getting washed and dressed and having breakfast as they prepared to go on market patrol, or in bed asleep after an arduous night duty, ran out of the station. All these police officers would have been struggling to get to grips with the facts of the case, what had happened, a description of the suspects and the threats that they posed. In the days before either force radios and still less personal radios this was quite a task, particularly as the officers would have had no experience of dealing with firearms incidents and the dangers that they posed.

Chesnut Road was a residential street with terraced houses on both sides. Most of these would have been shared by several families at this time. As Helfeld and Lepidus reached the bottom of Chesnut Road they found 12 housewives sitting in a circle. These women were wearing heavy wrap-around aprons with large metal bowls on their laps and they chatted and gossiped as they peeled the potatoes for their family's dinner. As the two robbers approached, chased by the local citizenry, the women stopped peeling and started throwing raw potatoes at them. It is highly likely that, in the chaos, a numbers of the pursuers would also have been struck by stray potatoes.

Helfeld and Lepidus had clearly decided to run through the housing estate, making many changes of direction and frequently turning to shoot at the people chasing them. After running down Chesnut Road, they turned left into Chesnut Grove, right into Scales Road then left into Dawlish Road and right into Mitchley Road where, outside the Mitchley Road Mission Hall, Helfeld, having presumably already fired the eight rounds in his weapon, stopped to reload it.

It was at this time that Joseph Wilson caught up with Helfeld and Lepidus in the car and was encouraged by PC Newman to use the vehicle to run them down. As both Helfeld and Lepidus had displayed their willingness to use their guns to kill in order to secure their escape, and at this point showed no signs of changing that policy so that they still posed a threat to the local citizenry, the use of the car as a weapon could be argued as being morally and legally justified. Helfeld and Lepidus managed to avoid being hit by the car and with their freshly-loaded weapons fired a hail of bullets at it. Mr Wilson swerved to avoid the bullets but at least three of them struck the vehicle; one passing through the front windscreen, shattering it and exiting out of the back of the vehicle, grazing Wilson's neck as it passed him. The second embedded itself in the rear upholstery, while the third hit the bonnet. The car crashed, injuring both Wilson and PC Newman and the car's radiator water pipe was riddled by gunfire, thus preventing any further use of it in the chase. Unfortunately, the hail of bullets also penetrated a car parked nearby and struck a ten-year-old baker's boy, Ralph John Joscelyne, who attended Earlsmead School, situated 0.7 mile/0.4 kilometre from the scene of the crime in Broad Lane, Tottenham. Ralph, hearing the gunfire, had been frightened for his safety and was hiding behind the car for cover.

Mrs Elizabeth Andrews, a leather cutter's wife of 4 Mitchley Road, hearing the gunshots, the police whistles and people shouting, rushed to her front door holding her baby. She saw the hail of bullets strike the car and young Ralph, and heard someone call out, "Oh my God! The boy is shot!" Handing her baby to a neighbour, she ran to assist Ralph, and stopped Wilson as he ran past and asked him to take the boy to the Prince of Wales Hospital in Tottenham Green East, formerly Tottenham Hospital (to which many statements, reports, etc. continued to refer) in the car, although she feared that the boy was already dead.

Joseph Wilson told Mrs Andrews that the car was out of action. Robert Skinner, a general dealer from nearby Junction Road, who had left his stock in Chesnut Road, had also seen Ralph fall. He hurried to lift the boy then handed him to Mrs Andrews, as he was too heavy for him to carry. William Dormer, a commercial traveller of 2 Dawlish Road was following the chase on his bicycle. Mrs Andrews stopped him and handed him

Ralph's body. While Mrs Andrews looked after his bicycle and retrieved her baby, Dormer carried the boy to the High Road. There where he was placed on a passing van and taken to the Prince of Wales Hospital, where it was confirmed that he was dead. Ralph had become the first casualty of the robbery. The baker whom Ralph had been helping had left him minding the horse and cart while he went to serve a customer. Upon his return, seeing that Ralph was absent, the baker assumed that he had joined in the pursuit of Helfeld and Jacob, and gave the matter no more thought. As a result it was only in the evening when Ralph failed to return home after helping the baker that his family started to make enquiries and learned of his death as recounted in *Chapter 9*.

Seeing Ralph killed and fearing that they could be killed too, Mr Schnurmann immediately took his two young assistants Allison and Keyworth back to the safety of the factory. Abandoning the damaged car, Wilson, Casewitz, and PCs Newman and Tyler joined the pursuing mob who had now caught up with the robbers, who had been delayed by their re-loading of their weapons, the attempt by Wilson to run them down, the subsequent car crash and the shooting of Ralph Joscelyne.

PC Bond then borrowed a small revolver from a member of the crowd and fired four shots at the fleeing robbers, but missed them completely. This then became a regular feature of the chase with a wide variety of people going home to collect weapons ranging from machine-guns, shotguns, rifles and pistols to swords, all of which were uncontrolled at the time and which they had collected whilst in the service of HM Forces in conflicts around the world.

The route from Chesnut Road to this point at Mitchley Road was built at the end of the 19th-century and is unchanged today. Mitchley Road is a continuous block of terraced housing and after this point the two robbers headed north which would have required them to turn left. Their only opportunity to do this would have been by turning into Junction Road. If they did that today they would run into five feet/1.52 metre high steel railings attached to the terraced houses at either end, behind which are garages and allotments accessed from the other side. Behind all this are now four rows of more modern terraced houses in Holcombe Road, Buller Road, Mafeking Road and Carew Road. Building on this new estate started in 1907, but was not finished until 1939 when the addresses appear in the Electoral Register for the first time. I am informed by the archivist at the Bruce Castle Heritage Centre that the development was abandoned for the duration of the First World War, re-opened a few years after the war, but was then damaged in the Second World War and the buildings were finally repaired and completed after the war. At the time of our story the area was largely open fields. As Lepidus and Helfeld ran across the fields their pursuers, lacking cover, would have had to hang back for safety.

Towards The Marshes...

Helfeld and Lepidus, having clearly decided to stay together, then ran down Dowsett Road into Down Lane (now part of Park View Road) and towards the recently-constructed Great Eastern Railway and The Marshes over the vast new cast iron footbridge at Down Lane Crossing. This would be a serious risk because the footbridge was of a close mesh construction, with high sides and just one opening at either end. For the several seconds that they were on the bridge they would be trapped like rats in a cage and provide an easy target for anybody wanting to snipe at them.

Knowing the area, and fearing that if Helfeld and Lepidus managed to cross the footbridge there was a chance that they would be lost forever in The Marshes, PCs Tyler and Newman attempted to cut them off by running across waste ground. The two groups were converging on the footbridge, each unaware of the other's presence due to a five feet/1.57 metre high fence surrounding the Dust Destructor (a large incinerator for domestic waste, and now a council waste depot). Finally, the four men were running alongside each other when the fence ended and they suddenly realised what was happening and turned to face each other. PC Tyler, an ex-soldier and the fitter of the two police officers, found himself face-to-face with the two robbers who had been running on the other side of the fence. He shouted "Come on; give in, the game's up." Helfeld took careful aim and shot PC Tyler through the head, before continuing to run away.

The entranceway to the Dust Destructor. Artist impression of how it looked at the time of the chase.

While cleaning the chicken house in his back yard, Mr Cubley, a mail porter, of Havelock Road, heard the commotion. His neighbour, Mrs Spedding, called to him: "There are two men coming with revolvers." Still wearing his house slippers, he ran out of his side garden gate just in time to see Helfeld shoot PC Tyler.

Unaware of PC Tyler's fate, Inspector Gould and Police Sergeant Hale were riding pedal cycles when they also recognised that the two robbers might be lost in The Marshes if they made it across the footbridge. A bystander, overhearing the officers' discussion told them that if the robbers were armed then they should be too and gave them his pistol. Taking the proffered pistol, the two police officers then made for the railway bridge as fast as they could.

At the same time, Mr Fowler, the superintendent of the Dust Destructor, hurried to its front gate where he met Sub-Divisional Inspector Large, who quickly informed him that two foreigners were running amok with firearms. At Inspector Large's request, Fowler agreed to use his telephone to call Stoke Newington Police Station, which unlike Tottenham Police Station had a telephone, to inform them of the situation. On receiving the message at Stoke Newington, Superintendent Jenkins responded by despatching all available men and horses to the scene. He then circulated details of the robbery to the six surrounding stations, seeking reinforcements. Next he set off in his car, accompanied by his groom and an armed PC in plain clothes, heading for Woodford, having been advised that Helfeld and Jacob were heading in that direction.

Firearms for the Police

Inspector Large then galloped swiftly back to Tottenham Police Station to obtain firearms. The gun cupboard was locked and nobody knew the location of the key as the weapons had never been needed before, so the cupboard was smashed open. Leaving the station and urging on his horse, Inspector Large galloped in the direction of the chase but failed to catch up again until the incident was all over.

A decision was then made to contact the gunsmiths in Holborn who usually sold weapons to the MPS and to seek their assistance; being public-minded citizens (and aware that the police were considering replacing their horde of weapons and would need to decide where to purchase these!) they readily agreed and quickly gathered together a selection of all the weapons that they stocked and which they might eventually supply to the police if they could be convinced of their usefulness. So it was that three taxi cabs were shortly filled with a range of weapons and ammunition from a machine gun to shotguns, rifles, pistols and revolvers—and despatched to Tottenham to join the chase.

There is a crossing-keeper's cottage next to the footbridge, but Walter Green was not at home at the time. His wife, Mrs Green was at home and she was outside sweeping. One of the robbers, probably Helfeld, grabbed her green cap from her head as he ran past. She resisted and the robber held a gun to her head but did not fire. The robber probably wanted the cap to disguise his appearance but just a few minutes later the police were instructing people to shoot at the man wearing the green cap and it nearly cost Helfeld, who was now wearing it, his life.

Shaken by her experience and probably needing a cup of tea, Mrs Green ran back inside the cottage as the two robbers made off towards the footbridge. As she stood at the kitchen window, filling her kettle, she saw the two robbers run off towards the footbridge, keeping up a constant barrage of fire. Then as they crossed it she saw Police Sergeant Hale arrive and take cover behind a telegraph pole next to Mr Wilkinson, the assistant to the council engineer, who had been supervising a party of unemployed men on culvert work, who hid behind another telegraph pole.

Into The Marshes...

Modern-day photograph of The Marshes.

As the robbers escaped the constraints of the iron bridge and entered The Marshes, they must have felt that their troubles were coming to an end. They were now leaving a well-policed residential area with crowds of market people and had travelled about 1.25 miles/2 kilometre in 25 minutes and, based on the rate of one shot every 22 seconds that they averaged over the entire pursuit, they would have fired around 67 rounds of ammunition. It is really rather surprising that they had only killed two people and injured just ten.

In front on them lay the vast open space that is The Marshes. Stretching ten miles by two was an area of scrubland ranging from what is now the 2012 Olympic Park in Stratford, through Hackney, Hackney Wick, Hackney Marsh, Clapton, Upper Clapton, Leyton, Lea Bridge, Walthamstow, Tottenham, Tottenham Hale, Blackhorse Road, Edmonton, Upper

Edmonton and Chingford, right up to Enfield Lock. Totally unmapped, largely unpoliced and unsuitable for road vehicles with a substantial number of reservoirs, lakes, ponds and puddles and a few railway lines cutting across it and frequented during the day by groups of men with shotguns shooting ducks, it was a vast wilderness with numerous natural obstacles and threats.

Late January in 1909 was typified by icy weather. As the *Daily Mirror* of January 24 reported, seven to ten degrees of frost were registered on the previous day and the thermometer had not risen above freezing point. The newspaper predicted a continuation of this and stated that dry, cold conditions prevailed throughout the south-east of England. The breath of both animals and humans clouded in the icy air as everyone went about their business on the morning of Saturday January 23. A strong wind turned all the weather vanes to the north-east, tore smoke from chimneys, and caused heavy grey clouds to scud across the dull, gloomy sky while creaking shop signs appeared in danger of being ripped from their hinges. Buffeted pedestrians fought with the bone-chilling wind trying to stop themselves being blown along by it. Those in cars were well wrapped-up, while in trams and buses passengers huddled together on the lower decks, leaving the open, empty upper-decks to the elements.

In this terrible weather the area could prove fatal. Certainly the robbers were not dressed to survive in these conditions. Perhaps the robbers thought that their pursuers would give up, but the reinforcements summoned by Superintendent Jenkins started to arrive from the surrounding police stations and converged on The Marshes. Some of these police officers were armed with official police weapons, some brought their own from home, some weapons they had borrowed; others were unarmed.

Having now completed his telephone call to Stoke Newington Police Station, Fowler, the superintendent of the Dust Destructor, was now making enquiries to find out what else he could do to assist in resolving the incident. He was told that PC Tyler had been shot and he collected the Dust Destructor's first aid kit and made his way to where PC Tyler had fallen. He bandaged his head wound and assisted PC Newman and Sub-Divisional Inspector Large, who had arrived on his horse, to carry PC Tyler to Oak Villa, a house in nearby Thackery Avenue. A doctor was summoned and the constable was taken by ambulance to the same Prince of Wales Hospital in Tottenham to which Ralph Joscelyne had been taken. He was alive on arrival, but died there five minutes later. The robbers had now claimed their second life during the robbery.

The Police Firearms arrive...

When the taxis containing the firearms arrived in Tottenham they had to stop and ask members of the public for instructions as to the current location of the chase so that they could deliver their weapons to the right place. Of course, when they reached the front of the chase and offered these, it was near the point of contact with the robbers and the police; shots were being fired and chaos was reigning. Some officers looked inside the taxis and were bemused by the choice available to them. Eventually they took a weapon that they thought most suitable for purpose and which they believed they could handle. There was no procedure to record what weapons had been taken by whom or to require the officers to sign for them. Presumably, there would have been no problem for a dishonest policeman to kill a robber, abandon the weapon that he had used in the river and deny any involvement. Possibly even worse, a dishonest officer could have killed an innocent bystander and disposed of the weapon and denied responsibility. Hopefully, there were no dishonest policemen on duty that day.

When all the policemen who wanted guns had chosen and taken them, there was still a good stock left in the taxis and members of the public started to help themselves and re-join the chase. Again there was no record of the issue nor any signatures accepting responsibility and the same possibilities for crime existed. It was not impossible that there were more Latvians living in "Little Russia" and that they could have used the weapons to join the chase on the Latvian side. Fortunately, there is no record of this occurring.

It is not known whether the gunsmiths had kept their own record of the weapons that they placed in the three taxis and just what proportion of the weapons were ever returned to them. Such knowledge might have concerned the local population and that of surrounding areas, if it had ever been broadcast.

At the point where they entered The Marshes, the robbers ran past what is now the Milmead Industrial Centre and the allotments and The Marshes opened up before them. They would have seen that there was a quarter mile flood plain separating Tottenham and Walthamstow. In quick succession there were Pymme's Brook, the River Lea Navigation (a canal), the River Lea, and a number of reservoirs. Of course the area was known as The Marshes, because it was all marshland; it was criss-crossed by numerous footpaths, but these were quite rough and this made running on them difficult. Only those who knew the area well would dare to venture away from the footpaths and attempt to walk on The Marshes themselves. They would have realised that it was going to be difficult finding a way through all these obstacles and would have started to understand the range of new problems that they faced.

Lepidus and Helfeld entered The Marshes on their western side. The police and civilians were behind them and even further west and the robbers therefore headed east to get away from them. The robbers would then have started to realise that with all the rivers, canals, reservoirs, streams, brooks and railway lines, running north to south that they would need to cross in order to make good their escape, they would have to zigzag wildly north and south in order to find bridges and fjords to cross these obstructions and escape to the east.

On entering The Marshes they headed north, leaping across Pymme's Brooke and crossing the River Lea Navigation at Stonebridge Lock. They were exhausted and took a break, but not a long one when they saw the police leading two teams of footballers towards them; asked by the police to assist in the chase the players readily agreed to briefly suspend the game. The robbers fired at the police and footballers and wounded three of them.

A party of sportsmen were shooting wild fowl around the edge of the Lockwood Reservoir. One of these men, Victor Albert Toley of Hanwell, later described their involvement in the chase to the *Wood Green Herald*:

"We heard a commotion on the marshes and looking over, saw a man in his shirt sleeves shooting with a revolver at two other men who were about 150 yards [137 metres] away. The two men were walking quite coolly and every few moments turned round to return the fire. Following the two men were a crowd of people including footballers who had been playing on the marshes, and police. When the police saw us they called out to us to shoot at the two men. Two of our party went across the stream and fired at the men with their sporting guns, but the range was too far for them to do any damage.

A Police Inspector called out 'Shoot at the man in the green cap'. We all tried a shot but they were too far away for our shots to be effective. We followed the two men and did not see them run at all. They were taking things quite coolly and keeping the crowd behind them at bay with their pistols. I said 'Come up here to the top reservoir and we shall cut them off'. We hurried up there and started firing at the men through the hedge, they being on the other side. They returned the fire. Most of us were lying down so they could not hit us and we aimed at their heads which we saw through the hedge. One of our men, who was standing up, had a bullet through his hat. We could not do much damage as we could not get a clear sight of them. We followed them through three fields and during this time we did not see them run at all. Their pursuers had to keep taking cover in order to escape their shots.

When we had first seen the crowd who were following them, there were only about five policemen and an Inspector among their numbers, but at the finish there were quite 100 constables who had hurried from all parts of the district."

One of the sportsmen had handed his gun to an ex-soldier named Woods, of Avenue Road, Edmonton, who had been in pursuit since the robbery in Chesnut Road. Woods fired unsuccessfully. Upon seeing one of the two men aim his gun at him, Woods took cover behind a fence, on the top of which he had rested his hat. A bullet passed through the fence close to it. Although the robbers continued to run, they had been seriously peppered by the buckshot from the duck-hunters' shotguns. Helfeld had injuries to his head and right arm so that when firing he had to use his left arm to steady his right arm, and Lepidus had to reload his weapon for him.

A modern revolver with modern ammunition may be effective at as much as 50 metres/55 yards today, but the user would have to aim the weapon a couple of metres above the target so that the trajectory of the bullet would bring it back down onto the target. A revolver from the turn of the century would not have made it that far and the bullets would have fallen well short. No wonder that the robbers were walking along quite coolly 150 metres away! A shotgun is a fiendish weapon, capable of cutting a man in half across his chest at less than 25 metres/28 yards, but of little use at distances above that, because the pellets spread and cause about the same damage, discomfort and inconvenience as an air rifle. The legality of the police instructing and inciting a member of the public to shoot, possibly to kill, men without giving any explanation as to their reasons for wanting them shot, is quite dubious. Police are sometimes required to stop people who pose a threat to life, but are seldom justified in shooting to kill, unless as in terrorist cases, they feel that the threat is so severe and so immediate that death is the only possible solution. In earlier times and the further one goes back the less such niceties were observed or questions asked perhaps, the less juries might be inclined to convict someone protecting property or disabling culprits.

The robbers found themselves trapped between the River Lea Navigation to the west and the River Lea on the east, with the police and footballers approaching from the south and therefore they had to head north-east in order to find a way across the river so that they could get to the eastern side of The Marshes and make good their escape. Taking the path which ran between the reservoirs, those following the robbers now faced even greater danger for the path was surrounded by high fences on both sides. With no opportunity to spread out, the pursuers had to keep close to the fence, all the time hearing shots ring out from the two men in front, some of which struck the fence palings. The robbers crossed the River Lea at the Chalk Bridge and immediately found themselves on the western edge of a reservoir.

Banbury Reservoir is a big bowl of water, approximately round in shape and with a diameter of approximately 800 metres/880 yards. It is surrounded by earthen banks 30 metres/100 feet high and topped with bushes and a fence. This is an area of open marshland and it is difficult to give locations so I will describe the robbers' route around the reservoir by noting positions according to a clock face, so that 12 o'clock is north, six o'clock is south, nine o'clock is west and three o'clock is east.

Once established on the far bank of the river, next to the reservoir, Helfeld and Lepidus rested before firing more shots at their pursuers, injuring two of the civilians. It was at this point that PC Nicod decided that enough was enough. Borrowing what he described as a "revolver" from a member of the public he crept ahead of the crowd through the reeds on the stream's banks and towards the two robbers, unobserved. Kneeling down on the bank of the river he took aim and squeezed the trigger, but nothing happened. Although he described the weapon as a "revolver" it may well have been a self-loading pistol and that the officer was unfamiliar with its safety catch and how it worked. In any event he was spotted by Helfeld and Lepidus who both fired at him as he beat a hasty retreat. He was hit twice in his left thigh and leg but subsequently recovered from his wounds. Around this time a young man called Cyril Burgess was wounded by a bullet, fired by one of the men, in the inner side of the right ankle.

As the robbers started to move north from Chalk Bridge they immediately came to a disused rifle range on their left. Starting from a point near the bridge the range spread out at 60 degrees for a mile-and-a-half/two kilometres to what was known as The Butts, a bank built up to stop the bullets at the end of the rifle range. The range was being demolishing by a gang of workmen. When they saw the robbers they gave chase and tried to stop them crossing the outfall channel at the Mill Stream Bridge. Once again the robbers got there first and kept the workmen at bay with a fusillade of shots, wounding two of them. Today the rifle range has been converted into two industrial estates, the Hastingwood Trading Estate and the Lea Valley Trading Estate.

The robbers then ran clockwise around the reservoir from nine o'clock to one o'clock where they crossed the Ching Brook as it joined the reservoir. As they reached the southern edge of the Banbury Reservoir, the robbers were confronted by Sidney Slater (aged 30), a horse-keeper, who had got ahead of the rest of the pursuers. The robbers fired six or seven shots at him and he was hit in the left thigh and disabled. First aid was rendered by the police and he was conveyed to the Prince of Wales Hospital. PC Spedding managed to get within 40 yards of the two robbers and fired four shots at them from a borrowed revolver, but they all missed.

Helfeld and Lepidus were now on the south slope of the reservoir. As they reached Folly Lane the robbers turned and fired upon their pursuers and Frederick Easter (aged 27) was shot, the bullet striking him on the left thigh and passing through the fleshy part of his left leg. He was taken to the Prince of Wales Hospital. They then ran down Folly Lane into Billet Road at the edge of the area known as Higham Hill where they burst through a gipsy encampment on the eastern side of the Lockwood Reservoir. The two robbers fired at anything that moved, scattering gypsies and stampeding ponies, but fortunately there were no casualties, human or equine. The robbers then continued down Billet Road towards the Crooked Billet Roundabout.

Seeing the mounting number of injuries, the courage of many of those who had been involved in the chase since the start began to fail and they retired and returned to Tottenham. But as the robbers reached the eastern edge of The Marshes and arrived at Salisbury Hall Farm, the site of Walthamstow Stadium in the years to come, just north of the Crooked Billet Roundabout on the Chingford Road, more police and civilians were waiting for them. On seeing them. The robbers took cover behind a haystack and kept their pursuers at bay with more or less continuous fire for several minutes. William Roker (aged 32) later described as "a local pugilist" who was "anxious to show his skill on the murderers," was shot in both legs and the others were pinned face down in the fields. He was conveyed to Walthamstow Cottage Hospital, where his condition was described as critical.

The Tram Chase

For now it was stalemate, but time was not on the robber's side. The police were starting to organize their response and gather the officers and weapons that they needed to bring this incident to a satisfactory conclusion. The farmyard abutted Chingford Road, along which the Walthamstow Urban District Council trams ran. By now Helfeld and Lepidus were getting extremely tired and decided to hijack a No.9 tram being driven along Chingford Road en route for the *Baker's Arms* in Lea Bridge Road. Tram driver Joseph Slow was driving the tram when he observed a throng of excited people rushing towards him and cries of "Stop! Murder!" He noticed that many in the crowd were firing weapons in the direction of two men and that several of the bullets narrowly missed him. The tram's conductor, Charles Wyatt, saw one of the men jump over the hedges that lined the fields. This man was carrying a pistol which he fired into the pursuing crowd. He leapt onto the tram's platform, all the time calling to a second man who was about 45 metres/50 yards behind who, as he ran, turned and fired at the pursuers. At this time there were only three passengers on the tram, a woman with a small son and an elderly gentleman, Edward Loveday (aged 63).

The robber on the tram, Lepidus, ordered Joseph Slow to stop the vehicle. He did so and fled to the upper deck, where he hid on the floor under one of the seats as bullets whistled all around him. He raised his head sufficiently to see that Wyatt had a pistol pressed to his face. Lepidus motioned with the gun to the conductor to start the tram, and said, "I ask you to drive on." At this, Loveday offered to leave the tram but, with another movement of the gun, Lepidus instructed him to stay on board. Wyatt told Lepidus that he had never driven a tram before but, seeing the determination on his face and uncomfortably aware of the warmth radiating from the gun barrel that pressed against his cheek, Wyatt sat in the driver's seat at the front of the tram. While still continuing to fire at the tram's pursuers, Helfeld had caught up and jumped on board. Wyatt started the tram and began to drive slowly through the hail of bullets whizzing past, showering the interior with shards of glass. To protect her son the woman passenger crouched with him on the floor.

Charles Wyatt drove on, constantly aware of the gun barrel pressed against his face. Occasionally, Lepidus would turn to fire at his pursuers, but he always returned the gun to Wyatt's cheek. Wyatt had another problem: he was afraid that Joseph Slow would endanger their lives by placing his weight against the overhead trolley bar, thus cutting off the electricity supply and bringing the tram to a standstill. As Wyatt slowed down at a loop to allow another tram to pass, the woman and her son scrambled off. Police Sergeant Hale stopped this other tram on the loop, telling the driver, "Follow that tram!" in reverse. About 40 police officers and several members of the public then climbed on board and the chase resumed with the occupants of both vehicles firing at each other, to little effect and with the police officers blowing their whistles.

Police Sergeant Hale and Inspector Gould also commandeered a car being driven by a chauffeur, Frederick Williams, to pursue the men. PCs Shakespeare and Gibb entered the vehicle while some of the crowd also swarmed aboard, hanging-on where they could. An advertising man's cart, taken over by PCs Williams and Hawkings (sometimes Hawkinges: who was armed with a double-barrelled shotgun) was gaining on the tram. As the cart drew close, Helfeld fired, bringing down the cart's galloping pony and overturning it, hurling its three occupants into the road where its contents of posters and paste landed on top of them. Having seen the fate of the advertising cart, and unaware of the other activity behind him, Wyatt continued to drive. All the time the chasing crowd grew in volume and bullets flew all around the tram as, clanking and swaying, it careered along at top speed. While he drove, the conductor prayed the two robbers would run out of ammunition, but they appeared to have an inexhaustible supply. No sooner were the chambers of their guns emptied than they reloaded from bullets kept in their pockets.

When they reached a turn in the road, Charles Wyatt had a brainwave. The quick-thinking conductor realising that the tram was, by its very nature, unable to change its course told Lepidus, who still held his pistol close to Wyatt's head, that there was a police station "just around the next corner." Lepidus replied that there was not. Unwilling to argue the point, Wyatt continued to drive. Just before the tram reached Kite's Corner, at the junction of Chingford Road and Farnham Road, Edward Loveday, who had become excited, attempted to rescue Wyatt. Lepidus fired his revolver at the old man, who fell, struck in the neck. But Wyatt's ruse worked and they instructed him to stop the tram at Kite's Corner where Helfeld and Lepidus dashed off looking for another means of escape.

Back to the Street Chase

They saw a milk cart standing at the kerb, its owner in a nearby harness maker's shop. They jumped on board and went to pull away. On hearing shouts that someone was interfering with his cart the milkman, George Conyard, jumped over the gate and challenged Helfeld and Lepidus. One of them shot Conyard in the arm and chest, then lashed the horse and took off in the direction of Epping Forest.

Joseph Slow had by now descended from the upper deck. Both he and Wyatt hoped they might intercept Helfeld and Lepidus, so Slow drove as fast as he could in the direction of *The Bell* public house, but the robbers had disappeared. When interviewed by *Lloyds News* after the pursuit, the driver of the second tram, Thomas J Carbolt, told the reporter that, as the vehicle containing Helfeld and Lepidus passed his tram on the loop, he was astonished to observe Wyatt driving and noticed Lepidus on the platform holding a gun to the conductor's head. He heard Lepidus shout at Wyatt: "Don't stop! Drive on!" and saw Helfeld on the rear platform maintaining continuous fire at the pursuing crowd. Wyatt later told reporters that when the tramcar was examined it was found to be riddled with bullets. His conclusion on the whole episode? "Never before have I had such an exciting time."

But milk carts are not built for speed, they are designed to keep all those bottles safe. The milk cart was overtaken by a horse and van being driven by a greengrocer's assistant, Thomas White and, as it passed them, one of the men pointed a gun at his head and he jumped off his seat. The two Latvians drove the milk cart along Farnham Road into Forest Road (next to Lloyd Park), where it crashed while negotiating a bend at speed. With a clanging of cans and milk pouring everywhere the cart overturned.

Abandoning the milk cart, Helfeld and Lepidus hijacked another horse and cart, with Lepidus riding the animal while Helfeld sat on the cart's tailboard with both pistols, maintaining a fusillade of bullets. By now those in pursuit included policemen on foot and on bicycles. One of the civilian cyclists brandishing a cutlass was the landlord of the *Crooked Billet* pub, who had rushed out to join the chase as it dashed past his premises, and who excitedly fired his gun.

Whenever anyone came close, Helfeld fired. In Forest Road he aimed at a policeman on foot, PC Adams. Uninjured, the policeman joined the chase, blowing his whistle all the while, then boarded the car which had earlier joined the pursuit.

Thomas Brown, upon hearing the shouting and being alerted to events by his small son was close on the robbers' heels. Helfeld fired at Brown, one shot whizzing past his right temple whilst another tore through the right leg of his trousers. As they drove, Helfeld took pot-shots at the crowd behind them. Police Sergeant Howitt and PC Francis were on point duty at Hagger Bridge when they heard shots and the sound of police whistles.

Today Hagger Bridge does not exist and several researchers have attempted to establish its location.

"The reference to Hagger Bridge probably refers to the stretch of Forest Road between Fulbourne Road and Hale End Road. This bridge, then as now, passes over the Liverpool Street to Chingford railway line. In all likelihood the Hagger name comes from the Hagger Farm which used to occupy the land on the north-east corner of the Wood Street/Forest Road/Fulbourne Road crossroads." (Barry Ryder (2015). See http://www.walthamstowmemories.net/pdfs/BarryRyder-TottOutrage.pdf)

Police Sergeant Howitt and PC Francis both attempted to stop the horse and cart, but jumped aside when several shots were fired at them by the robbers. One bullet passed between the two policemen and shot out the side window of a shop at 849 Forest Road, which since 1952 has operated as Cogger's Florists. However, the actions of the police officers caused the horse to swerve off the road and it crossed some waste land into Fulbourne Road, and thence into Wadham Road, now part of the North Circular Road.

Thomas Brown was not intimidated by the shots that the robbers had fired at him, but he may well have been aggravated by them, because he had then jumped into the car with the police officers and played an active role in the remainder of the chase. Also in the car was a man with a breech-loading gun. The vehicle followed the greengrocer's cart, moving close when the armed passenger wanted to fire. Eventually the armed man left the vehicle, handing the weapon and some cartridges to Brown, who fired at the robbers in Wadham Road. The road increased in steepness causing the weary horse to slow. Dissatisfied with the speed that the horse and cart was achieving despite their frenzied lashing of the horse, and unaware that one of the cart's wheels was secured by a chain brake and was therefore sliding rather than rolling across the road, the two robbers abandoned the horse and cart in Winchester Road. Onlookers saw Helfeld hand his companion one of the weapons

Helfeld is Captured

Having abandoned their vehicle in Winchester Road, Lepidus and Helfeld were dirty, exhausted and bleeding from gunshot wounds and grazes. They made their way to the railway arch that runs across the Ching Brook, dashed down the slope to the brook and ran along the footpath, unaware this converged into 1.83 metre/six feet high fence that formed the boundary of houses on a newly built estate. All the while, shots were being fired at Helfeld and Lepidus and it was obvious to their pursuers that they were on the verge of collapse. Realising their error and cornered, they could go no further. Lepidus, the taller of the two, managed to struggle over the fence; Helfeld, unsurprisingly for a man known to his friends as "Elephant" was the stockier of the two and unable to haul himself it and stumbled and fell. Witnesses later reported hearing Helfeld call to Lepidus: "Go on, save yourself. I've only got two left." With this, Helfeld took a final shot at the approaching crowd before using his last bullet to shoot himself in his right eye. Helfeld survived the initial injury and continued to struggle violently.

Winchester Road railway arch, known locally as "Assassin's
Alley" (inset photograph believed to be of Henry North).

Helfeld was enthusiastically overpowered by his pursuers, who went
on to rather violently express their annoyance at his actions. His head
wound was roughly dressed with strips torn from his shirt and a van was
quickly requisitioned to take him to the same Prince of Wales Hospital
in Tottenham as his two victims. While being driven there, accompanied by police, he did not speak, beyond mumbling that he was cold.

The first policeman to reach Helfeld was PC Shakespeare. He picked
up the gun which had fallen from Helfeld's hand and handed it to DC
Dixon, who had cycled from Edmonton Police Station. The detective
resumed the chase, saying that he would use the gun for a shot at "the
other one." If Helfeld had been correct a minute or two earlier when he
had said, "I've only got two left," perhaps Dixon should have checked
that the weapon was still loaded before relying on it to confront Lepidus?

Lepidus is Cornered

Having scaled the fence and heard his friend shoot himself, Lepidus then faced the steep incline that led to the railway, scrambling for a foothold all the way. Crossing the railway lines he ran down the other side to land where house building was in progress, leaping over piles of bricks and timber while still being chased by both civilians and police, including Police Sergeant Hart and PC Zeithing. Lepidus turned and fired: one bullet passed over PC Zeithing's left shoulder and entered the chest of builder Frederick Mortimer, who had thrown a brick at Lepidus, which missed its target. Lepidus also fired another two shots at PC Zeithing, one of which passed through the lapels of his greatcoat.

Still firing, Lepidus made his way from Beech Hall Road towards fields bordering Prestons Avenue. At the top of that avenue stood a public house, the *Royal Oak*. Crossing Hale End Road to the rear of the *Royal Oak*, Lepidus crept along behind a hedge bordering a row of cottages. Thomas Brown, who had accompanied the police following Lepidus, observed his progress and took aim but did not fire. Chased by Police Sergeant Hart, Lepidus leapt the hedge of Oak Cottage.

Oak Cottage was a small two-storey house consisting of four rooms and a lean-to, occupied by Charles Rolstone, a coal carrier, his wife Eliza, a washer woman, and their two sons. Mr Rolstone was not at home at this time, and unaware of events at the rear of his home, and attracted by the sound of all the shouting, the police whistles and guns firing, Mrs Roleston ran to the front gate, leaving her sons alone inside the house, to see what was happening. A policeman ran past, curtly ordering her and all the others drawn outside by the commotion to go back into their homes and lock their doors as there was a murderer on the loose. Mrs Rolstone turned to go inside but found both the front door and the door to the lean-to locked. As she struggled with the lean-to door she was horrified to see a man's face with wild eyes stare back at her through a window at the side of the house. The face was covered in blood from wounds probably caused by pellets from the shotguns fired at the man during the chase.

Upon seeing the intruder in her home, Mrs Rolstone shrieked, "Oh, my children! My children!" Inside the house they could be heard screaming. In the back yard the family dog, a collie bitch called Nell, chained to a wall, jumped up and down and barked furiously.

Sightseers at Oak Cottage

The large mob quickly converged on the cottage and surrounded it. Lepidus had no way out. Outside the cottage, Police Sergeant Hart saw the large crowd of local people and police officers gathering; he saw the horde of weapons that they held, ranging from guns to long metal poles and heavy chunks of wood; he knew that Lepidus was well-armed; he recognised the potential danger to all concerned if this became an all-out battle. He knew that the Rolstone children were in the house and that they could be used by Lepidus as hostages. He took control of the scene and instructed everybody to wait outside.

Lepidus, once inside the cottage, locked all the doors and windows and frantically attempted to climb the large, old fashioned chimney of the front parlour fireplace. Possibly hoping to escape over the roofs of the adjoining cottages and to use the roofs as a vantage point in a gun battle, or just hoping to hide there and get his breath back. After a few minutes, he gave up his attempt and brought down a deluge of soot. This was witnessed by the Rolstone's middle child, Charles, then aged six. Lepidus then swigged water from a jug left for the children and threatened the youngest with being shot if he did not stop crying, shouting, "Stop that noise!" His sooty, blood-smeared face was later seen peering around a curtain in the front bedroom. Upon sight of him, a fusillade of shots shattered the window panes and many of the cottage's contents. Thomas Brown was one of those who fired. Lepidus returned fire. Three times he was called upon to surrender but each time his response was another volley of bullets.

Realising that, with Lepidus upstairs, the two boys were alone on the ground floor, PC Dewhurst and Charles Schaffer, who had been in on the chase from the start, managed to force open the door to the lean-to and crept into the kitchen where they found the two boys and brought them out of the cottage to safety.

Three young police officers appear to have taken the initiative in dealing with Lepidus at this stage. None of them had been heard of previously in the chase and they seem to have decided that it was necessary to kill Lepidus, and ruthlessly set about trying to do this. The leader of these officers appears to have been PC 636 "J" Charles Eagles. He was a Walthamstow officer, who had been sent to investigate an incident at Walthamstow Waterworks, where a policeman was believed to have been shot. Arriving at the waterworks, he was informed that the incident was at Wood Street so he cycled there, where he was directed to Oak Cottage. Coming from another division he would have been unlikely to know any of the Tottenham officers. For some unknown reason he was in plain clothes; he may well have been posted to winter patrols, which were the way for ambitious young officers to draw attention to themselves and secure selection to the CID. Despite his prominent role in bringing the chase to a satisfactory conclusion, nothing more was heard of PC Eagles after The Outrage.

DC Charles Dixon was a member of a small CID unit attached to Tottenham Police Station. As such he would have been dressed in plain clothes like the others. He appears to have been happy to allow PC Eagles to take the initiative and to support him. When PC Eagles asked DC Dixon for his police service pistol, he gave it to him and took another weapon for himself.

Police Constable 741 "N" John William Cater was a 29-year-old married man attached to Tottenham Police Station, with eight years police service behind him. At the time of the robbery he was off duty in plain clothes wearing a Guernsey jumper, in the married quarters next to Tottenham Police Station. Clearly, having covered over six miles, he would have been pretty tired, which may be why he allowed the fresher PC Eagles to take the lead. Also at the cottage was Inspector Gould. His role there has never been fully explained, but he was the senior officer present and would have been expected to take a strong lead. It would appear from the comments that do exist that he set himself up as the incident commander, initially outside the cottage, later moving inside when circumstances permitted. Certainly, the officers at the scene do appear to return to him to discuss developments and future action.

As soon as he knew that the children were safe, PC Eagles borrowed a breech-loading shotgun from a bystander and entered the cottage to search for Lepidus. While in the scullery he heard Lepidus upstairs and realising that if he followed him up the narrow staircase he would present a perfect target for him, he decided to leave the cottage and seek another solution.

Back on the ground, PC Eagles explained to his colleagues about Lepidus being upstairs and the narrow staircase being the only way up after him, and the three police officers went to find a ladder. Fortunately, they quickly found one at the next door cottage and put it up against the back bedroom window. PC Eagles then got rid of the shotgun, which was far too long and unwieldy if he was to climb the ladder, and borrowed a pistol (which Superintendent Jenkins in his closing report again wrongly describes as being a revolver) from a member of the crowd. Meanwhile, Police Sergeant Hart searched the lower part of the house with the Rolstone family dog, Nell, that he had found tied up outside and he then sent her upstairs (In his report Superintendent Jenkins mistakenly attributes this action to Dixon).

PC Eagles, holding his pistol, slowly ascended the ladder and, upon reaching the top, cautiously opened the window. He saw the dog enter the front bedroom and tried to persuade it to go under the bed to see if Lepidus was hiding there. It was then that he saw Lepidus framed in the bedroom doorway pointing a gun at him. He tried firing his gun but could not make it work, probably due to a safety catch and so descended the ladder far more rapidly that he had ascended it!

Interestingly, the MPS did not have police dogs at this time, but the previous year, in 1908, the *Police Review* noted that

> "[T]he authorities at Scotland Yard have been seriously discussing the use of dogs as the constable's companion and help, and Sir Edward Henry [Commissioner], who regards the innovation sympathetically, considers the only crucial objection to be the sentimental prejudices of the public."

The three officers held another brief conference with Inspector Gould and, as keenly aware as they were that if Lepidus fired at them on the narrow staircase they would have no chance of escape, they decided that they had no practical alternative. Gould sought a volunteer to lead the charge up the stairs to confront Lepidus and if necessary kill him. PC Eagles was prepared to go in the lead, but only if he was supplied with a service revolver, with which he was familiar and which he was confident would work well. Gould then instructed DC Dixon to hand over a service revolver in his possession and ensured that DC Davies had another weapon. It is unclear whether DC Dixon had somehow come into possession of two service revolvers, or whether he already had another weapon, or whether PC Eagles gave him the semi-automatic pistol that he had been unable to fire in exchange for the service revolver, but whatever DC Dixon was still himself armed after giving PC Eagles a service revolver.

Four armed men then entered the cottage through the front door. In the lead, as agreed, was PC Eagles. He was followed, in order, by DC Dixon, PC Cater and Thomas Brown the civilian. Brown lived in Forest Road, Walthamstow and had been present when Helfeld shot himself. In his statement, shown in full at *Appendix 2* to this work, Brown states that PC 747 Shakespeare then took possession of Helfeld's weapon and continued to pursue Lepidus. Brown then jogged over to the officer and asked him if he could have the gun and the officer gave it to him. Forensic evidence was not as important in 1909 as it is today and the officer was not concerned at losing any fingerprint, DNA or firearms evidence to show that Helfeld had shot himself rather than having been shot by the police or public chasing him. In her book, *Outrage, An Edwardian Tragedy,* the author, J D Harris states that Helfeld's weapon was picked up by a PC Shakespeare. He is then said to have handed it over to DC Dixon. Of course, it may be Dixon, who took possession of it at the scene of Helfeld's shooting and who was another of the men to enter the cottage with Brown, may have handed to him.

Suspecting Lepidus may have sneaked downstairs and attempted to scale the parlour fireplace once again, the men fired a shot up the chimney, dislodging even more soot. After this, DC Dixon carefully opened the door to the stairs and called on Lepidus to surrender, but there was no reply. Next the four men cautiously ascended the staircase.

Upon reaching the small landing at the top of the stairs, the men saw feet under the closed front bedroom door and realised that Lepidus was facing them through it. PC Eagles fired twice and PC Cater once, through the door. All was quiet within, then the policemen heard a shot come from within the room. The officers forced their way in and found Lepidus on the bed "in the throes of death" with his gun in his hand beside him. He was bleeding from a wound in his right temple, lying on a small, bloodstained bed. PC Eagles took his gun from his hand. Lepidus was carried into the back garden where within minutes he was dead.

To ensure he was not shamming, Police Sergeant Hart gently nudged him with his foot; there was no response. At the time PCs Eagles and Dixon thought that one of the three shots that they had fired through the door at Lepidus must have been fatal, but at the inquest into his death on 26 January 1909 the coroners court heard that the bullet that killed him had been of the same calibre as Lepidus' own weapon, and different from that of the weapons held by the officers. Pursuers and sightseers crowded the back garden, eager to view the corpse.

Lepidus was examined by a Dr Alcock, who had been attending a patient nearby, who pronounced him dead and expressed his opinion that death had been due to the bullet wound to the head. Lepidus was taken by police ambulance to the mortuary at Queen's Road, Walthamstow where, on being undressed, hundreds of shotgun pellets fell from his clothes. When the body was searched, it was found that as well as his gun, Lepidus had carried a dagger, embossed in German with the words *Gib uns heute unser tägliches Brot* ("Give us this day our daily bread") on its handle and with *Himmel* ("Heaven") on its blade. Also in his possession were four home made magazine cases, bullets of the soft-nosed, dum-dum variety and two paper money bags, one of which contained £5 in silver, the other one empty. There was no sign of the remaining £75.

The chase had lasted two and a half hours and covered some six-and-a-half miles. Around 1,000 members of the public and 100 police officers had joined it at various times. The two Latvians had used every one of their 400 rounds of ammunition, been responsible for four deaths, those of one police officer, one boy and each of their own (as we shall see in *Chapter 9*, Helfeld was to die in hospital).

With so many private weapons involved in the incident, it is impossible to calculate just how many were employed by the chasers, but with 400 rounds being fired towards them and so many weapons available to all and sundry, it is unlikely that they fired less than the robbers. My best estimate would be that the chasers fired around 600 rounds of ammunition at the robbers, this is probably the only gunfight in England in which over 1,000 rounds of ammunition were discharged in all, and probably one of only a very few incidents in the world when this has happened, if ever before or afterwards.

CHAPTER 8

The Claims

A few days after the robbery, Home Secretary Herbert Gladstone formally declared The Tottenham Outrage to have been a riot. This was an admission that the government had failed to enforce the King's Peace and properly protect the public and, that as a consequence, it was responsible for all the damages and costs incurred by citizens as a result of its failure. Opening the cash registers in this way encouraged every budding entrepreneur to consider the ways in which he or she had suffered financially so that they could submit a claim and make some money. Over 30 claims for compensation, for damage and injury, were received.

The MPS had received a great deal of support and assistance from the public during and after The Outrage, but at the end of the day, they were still basically civil servants and they set about scrutinising every claim for compensation rigorously, without showing any appreciation for the public's support, or any sympathy. Claims for even relatively small amounts were closely examined at each level of the MPS chain of command, up to and including the commissioner, and then forwarded on to the Home Secretary for final approval.

George Smith, the gas stoker shot in the course of the robbery at the Schnurmann's Rubber Factory, claimed for the bullet holes to his overcoat and cap, inflicted as he struggled with Lepidus and Helfeld and attempted to detain them. Smith was 40-years-old and lived with his wife and six dependent children at 17 Hartington Road, Tottenham. As Helfeld and Lepidus ran off towards Mitchley Road, Smith had been taken inside Tottenham Police Station and treated by the police surgeon for his bullet wounds, which were later described as being just grazes. Smith was so tough that just a few hours later he went to work as usual, on night duty. He later remarked bitterly that if some of the other bystanders had attempted to apprehend the two robbers rather than just watching them, the whole tragedy may have been averted. Smith claimed £2 for the damage to his clothing. Four weeks' wages, bearing in mind that the average pay due to each of the employees at Schnurmann's was just ten shillings (50p).

In direct contrast to the robust George Smith, the next claim was made on behalf of George Dawkins. Dawkins, aged 41, lived with his wife and two children, aged ten and three, at 3 Kings Place Road, Buckhurst Hill and was employed as a carman (the driver of a horse and cart: the "white van man" of today) by builders, W & C French, also of Buckhurst Hill. Dawkins claimed that he had been driving his brick cart with his pal Charles Brown of Albert Cottages as a passenger. As they approached Salisbury Hall Farm they had seen the crowds in hot pursuit of Helfeld and Lepidus and saw the two robbers mount the tram. Dawkins and Brown followed the chase at a distance until it reached the *Victory* public house (now the *Dog and Duck*) at 222, Chingford Road. Despite never getting closer than 640 metres/700 yards from the robbers, the two men had felt obliged to enter the public house and soothe their ruffled nerves with half-a-pint of ale. Apparently, after leaving the public house Dawkins had laid down in the bottom of his cart and covered his head with a horse rug. He had remained there until they reached Whipps Cross when Brown said that Dawkins had told him his head felt "queer."

After the robbery, Dawkins' behaviour continued to be strange and his family claimed that he had not been "right in the head" since. At one point it was feared he might need to enter an asylum. Although not legally obliged to do so, his employers took the view that Dawkins had been working for them when this had happened and paid reduced wages to his wife and children and also his medical fees. The company then submitted a claim to the police for compensation for his medical expenses, his loss of earnings and the price of the ale that he had consumed, but after careful and prolonged consideration this particular claim was disallowed. After a period of time Dawkins gradually improved and was able to resume his life and work. It is ironic that whilst George Smith (above) engaged the robbers in mortal combat and they repeatedly aimed shots at his head and torso, he continued to work as usual, but that his name-sake who never got closer to the robbers than 640 metres/700 yards had a nervous breakdown.

The most complex claim was the one made by Aldred Brothers of Longfellow Road, Walthamstow. Their pony had been shot in the ten-dons of its hind leg and they claimed for veterinary treatment, two or three hours of daily care for the pony while it recovered, the hire of a replacement pony to allow them to continue in business, and the depre-ciation in the value of the pony as a result of its wounds. Sub-Divisional Inspector Gray was deputed to investigate the claim. Gray discovered that it had been considerably inflated. Apparently, a veterinary surgeon had expressed the opinion that the pony had only required one hour of daily care, rather than the two or three hours each day that had been claimed for. He also discovered that the Aldred Brothers had paid Hor-ace Rumsey, a local pawnbroker ten shillings (50p) for the hire of a replacement pony, rather than the £1 that they had claimed (£1 in 1909 equals £108 in 2017). He also challenged a claim by Aldred Brothers that they had paid another ten shillings to have the damaged van removed on a trolley. John Aldred, claimed £3 3 shillings (£3.15) for deprecia-tion in the animal's value. However, a vet put the value of the animal at "about £10" and stated that "it had been worth £12 before it received its injury... [although] a shock of this kind would tend to make the animal unreliable and likely to take fright at street noises." Gray recommended that the Aldred claim be reduced to reflect these issues. Senior officers adjudged that Aldred's had made a false claim for vet's fees and exagger-ated the depreciation in the value of the animal. After some negotiation, a reduced claim was settled. A figure of £2 10 shillings (£2.50) was even-tually agreed for the depreciation of the animal.

Following on from the shooting of the pony, Arthur Rowntree of West Green School, Tottenham had allowed PC 50 "N" R Hawkings to borrow his bicycle to continue his pursuit of the robbers when the pony pulling his cart had been shot from under him. Unfortunately the bicycle had been damaged whilst being used by the officer and Rowntree claimed 3/9d for the repairs.

Most of the casualties from The Outrage had been taken to the Prince of Wales Hospital in Tottenham Green East. Helfeld had been detained there after the incident until he died. For two weeks rigorous security arrangements had been put in place to ensure his security and prevent his escape. This had seriously inconvenienced the hospital and its staff and Sir Edward Henry recommended, and the Home Secretary approved, an ex gratia payment for the inconvenience, but only on condition that it was made clear to the hospital that this was a one-off, exceptional payment.

There was also a range of minor, but interesting claims:

- The Down Lane Crossing keeper's wife, Mrs Lizzie Green claimed for her green cap which had been snatched from her head by one of the gunmen, who probably wanted to use it as a disguise. This may have been a bad decision, because as explained earlier as they entered The Marshes, the police were telling duck shooters to aim at the man in the green cap. The cap might have kept a robber's head warm, but it could easily have led to his death too.

- Thomas Brown of 11 Albion Road, Walthamstow, who had taken part in the chase and joined the posse of officers who went upstairs in Oak Cottage to face Lepidus, claimed 12/6d for damage caused to his trousers by a bullet.

- Mr Thorogood, a shunter with the Great Eastern Railway and the resident of Oak Villa, Thackeray Avenue, Tottenham, where the dying PC Tyler had been carried after being shot, claimed £1.10.0 in respect of an overcoat, a table cover and three pieces of carpet that had been damaged by Tyler's blood. Superintendent Jenkins supported the claim, stating that all the items listed had been on the ground floor of Mr Thorogood's home where there had been "considerable damage."

- George Cousins, a 29-year-old casual market porter living with his wife and three dependent children at 14 Asplins Road, Tottenham claimed 12/- (60p) for damage to his clothing.

- George Harwood, a 26-year-old labourer living with his wife and one dependent child at 6 Park Lane, Tottenham had the fingers of his right hand wounded at the railway bridge by Jacob Lepidus as he was making his escape. He claimed 5/- (25p) for damage to his clothing.

- Sidney Slater, a 30-year-old unemployed horse keeper living with his wife and six dependent children at 6 Eaton Place, Fore Street, Edmonton had been shot in his left thigh at Higham Hill. He claimed £1 for damage to his clothing.

- William Roker, a 32-year-old unemployed plasterer's labourer living with his wife and three dependent children at 4 Cross Street, Angel Road, Edmonton had been shot in both legs at Salisbury Hall Farm. He was to have taken part in a boxing match at the Municipal Buildings just two days after The Outrage, on 25 January. He was visited in hospital by a police superintendent, who found him to be: "An industrious man who does work when he can get it, which recently has been but casual. He is a total abstainer and is known locally as a pugilist." Police at Edmonton Station raised £1 for his wife and children. He claimed 12/- for damage to his clothing.

- Frederick Mortimer, a 38-year-old master plasterer living with his wife and seven dependent children at 18 Palmerstone Road, Walthamstow had been shot in the chest on both sides. He claimed £2 for damage to his clothing.

- During the chase, PCs William Shakespeare and George Gibb commandeered a car, registration number LN 1662 belonging to Ferdinand and Edward Reiss, of St Julians, Hampstead Road, Walthamstow and driven by their chauffeur, Frederick Hulme Williams. The car had been damaged when several members of the public clambered onto the back of it and bent both of its rear wings. The police had to pay £1.1.0 (£1.05) for damage for repairs to the bodywork.

- George White, a greengrocer of Chingford Road, Walthamstow had his cart stolen by the robbers and claimed £2.10.0 (£2.50) in respect of lost earnings after having to rest his pony for four days when the animal became overstrained, and his son Thomas White, who had been driving the cart, suffered severe shock and was unable to work for the same period.

- Interestingly, Charles Rolstone, the coal porter, who lived in Oak Cottage in Hale End (*Chapter 8*), a two-up-two-down worker's cottage and the venue of the final shoot-out, made a claim for £10 in respect of the damage caused to the cottage. He appears to have made no reference to the fact that the Lepidus may well have left a black bag with £80, the proceeds of the robbery, up his chimney, whilst he was there (*Chapter 9*). Surprising that, if so.

- Finally, even Superintendent Jenkins himself made a claim for £5.10.0 (£5.50) although there is no record of what he actually claimed for.

All the claims are set out in full in the official schedule prepared by Superintendent Jenkins, and re-produced in *Appendix 9*.

The Aftermath

As the woefully cold and dull day of The Outrage faded to gloomy dusk, the street-lighter made his way along Arnold Road, stopping at every lamp post and resting his bicycle against it while with his long pole he ignited the gas lamps that brought light to the Tottenham streets. Inside No.32, Mrs Emily Tyler watched the man's slow progress from her parlour window, trying to quell the anxiety arising from her husband's extreme lateness in coming home for his mid-day meal. This stood on a saucepan of water that had several times boiled dry. In nearly six years of marriage, she had become accustomed to the erratic nature of police work, but today he was later than ever.

Just after 4 p.m. Harry Jelley, a friend of the Tylers called on Mrs Tyler, where he was surprised to learn that she had no knowledge of her husband's whereabouts and nobody from the police station had thought to inform her of what had happened. Trying to break the news gently, Jelley told her that her husband had been involved in a bit of "bother" near the police station, that he had heard PC Tyler had been shot in the leg and that a constable who was possibly PC Tyler had been taken to the Prince of Wales Hospital.

Assuming they were going to visit her husband in hospital, Mrs Tyler hurriedly put on her coat and hat and accompanied Mr Jelley but, upon seeing a crowd at the top of Arnold Road, he took her in the opposite direction. Mrs Tyler wanted to go directly to the hospital to make enquiries after her husband, but Mr Jelley persuaded her to wait until the crowd had dispersed and suggested that she accompany him to his home in nearby Wakefield Road. There, in the presence of his own wife, Jelley broke the news of her husband's death to Mrs Tyler. She did not return home but stayed with the Jelley's until the day of the funeral.

Unaware that the police were searching for the family of an unidentified boy who had been shot earlier that day, and due to their son's non-appearance, anxiety was mounting at Ralph Joscelyne's home. It was not until 7 p.m. that a policeman called on the Joscelynes. He showed the worried parents a necktie and asked them if they recognised it: Ralph's mother immediately did so, as belonging to her son. His parents went with the policeman to the Prince of Wales Hospital and identified Ralph's body.

As always, one of the first consequences of a major incident is the arrival of the media with their efforts to find a "story." As the robbery had occurred on a Saturday there were two sets of journalists wandering around Tottenham in the hours after it, one from the Sunday papers and one from the daily newspapers wanting a follow-up piece for Monday. Of course, there was no television at this time, but as a consequence radio had a far higher profile and spread the story ahead of the newspapers coming out.

By the next day, Sunday 24 January 1909, news of The Outrage had spread throughout London. Undeterred by the cold weather, loaded brakes, cars and other vehicles brought thousands from all over the capital to view the route of the chase. Over 100 extra police officers were drafted in to control the crowds and keep them moving; the same number that had been involved in the incident itself. There was no trouble, the sightseers were orderly. Some were content to throng outside Schnurmann's Rubber Factory or view the spot where PC Tyler had fallen, while others visited the homes of PC Tyler and Ralph Joscelyne. The police conducted a thorough search of the route and hundreds of members of the public walked it picking through gardens in the hope of finding some of the missing money.

In Essex, similar numbers from London and elsewhere went to the railway bridge where Helfeld had been captured and flocked to Oak Cottage. Because of the huge numbers many public houses, including the *Royal Oak*, soon ran out of beer and had to call for further supplies. Charles Rolstone, the occupant of Oak Cottage, was never a man to miss an opportunity. He placed a glass dish in his hallway labelled "For the Children" and encouraged visitors to place their donations in there before he took them on a guided tour of his home and showed them the damage inflicted on the cottage by the shoot-out. Oak Cottage was in a sorry state. The furniture and walls were spattered with blood and sooty handprints and, like the doors, were pocked with bullet holes while smashed ornaments lay on the floor with glass from the shattered windowpanes. The front parlour, with its damaged portrait of Queen Victoria hanging crookedly over the mantelshelf, and the metal fender in front of the fireplace bent from where Lepidus had stood on it, was buried under a pall of soot.

Also on the Sunday, Superintendent Jenkins took the Commissioner of the MPS, Sir Edward Henry around the route of the chase in his car. Sir Edward expressed his approval of the prompt way in which the local police had reacted to the incident and announced his intention of attending the officer's funeral. On the Monday, feelings ran high at Schnurmann's and other local factories that employed immigrant labour and threatening language was used. Police officers were posted to these premises to deter possible disorder, but there was none. Rumours circulated that anarchists planned to bomb the Prince of Wales Hospital where Helfeld lay; the police presence there was doubled and armed.

Much of this hysteria could be attributed to the press: On Monday 25 January 1909 the *Daily Mirror* devoted its whole front page to photographs of 13 of the dead and injured. These appeared under a double headline, "Murderous Outbreak of Russian Anarchists in London: Three Killed, Many Injured. Heroic Policemen among the Slain." Many papers also carried articles blaming lax administration of the Aliens Act, and several queried the efficiency of police firearms training and out-of-date weaponry.

On Tuesday, 26 January 1909, the same newspaper alleged that an English shopkeeper had said that many of the aliens living in the High Cross Road, "Were of no use to anybody. Here and there you find a decent man or woman but nearly all of them are downright riff-raff" and the next day it reported that: "Inquiries in the alien quarter of Tottenham (near the Prince of Wales Hospital) yesterday showed that the majority of Russians there could not write their name in English. Till the (workhouse) guardians and the police co-operated to put an end to the practice, the aliens used to sleep twelve to twenty to a room." A common belief of the time was that aliens were taking jobs from Englishmen by undercutting wages and were prepared to pay more for inferior accommodation. Yet paradoxically, they were perceived as lazy and not prepared to work. In the press and popular literature aliens were accused of being insanitary and dishonest, of interbreeding and of degenerate behaviour as well as many other vices or crimes. Following The Outrage, throughout London many people whose appearance was even slightly foreign were beaten up, even if they were of English origin.

The local body of anarchists in Tottenham, the Lettish Social Democratic Party, probably fearing for their own safety, wasted no time in disassociating themselves from the two robbers, repudiating any connection with them and denying that they had ever had any association with the Lettish Revolutionary Party. They then went on to express their deep regret at the deaths of PC Tyler and Ralph Joscelyne.

The bodies of Tyler and Ralph Joscelyne lay in Tottenham Mortuary. By Monday evening the coffins they were to occupy had been placed in the window of J Seaward (Undertakers) of High Cross, Tottenham, who had expressed their intention of not accepting payment for the two funerals, which were to take place on Friday, January 29.

On Monday 25 January 1909, two days after the robbery, Sir Edward Henry submitted a special report for King Edward VII. The King responded the next day with a personal note prepared by an equerry in which he expressed his thanks to Henry for the "interesting and graphic account of the tragedy at Tottenham" and offered his opinion that, "It is almost inconceivable that such a thing could have occurred in these days on the very outskirts of London. The King thinks that the police behaved with great gallantry and should you consider it desirable to do so, he would be glad if you would convey to those engaged in the affair, and especially the (two) [sic] officers who entered the house, his high appreciation of their conduct."

On Wednesday 27 January 1909, just four days after the robbery, the King expressed his sympathy in the following terms:

"The Commissioner is commanded to convey to the police officers engaged in the tragedy at Tottenham the King's high appreciation of their gallant conduct. His Majesty also directs that the expression of his sincere sympathy may be communicated to the widow and family of Police Constable Tyler, killed while courageously doing his duty."

The Inquests

Unusually, two separate inquests were held for those who died in The Outrage. Today this would be considered unnecessary duplication of effort and an unwarranted expense as many witnesses would be required to appear at two different courts in order to give the same evidence to two different coroners. There would also be concern that the two coroners could make conflicting rulings and arrive at different verdicts and thereby attract criticism. Today it would all be considered a single event and if two coroners were involved to start with they would get together and decide which of them should hear the case, unless it was considered to be of such a high profile that a High Court judge should be appointed to hear it.

PC Tyler and Ralph Joscelyne had both died early in the chase within the area of the Tottenham coroner, while the two perpetrators had died at the end of the chase within the jurisdiction of the Walthamstow coroner and this is the way that the inquests were arranged. By the time they opened at Tottenham and Walthamstow on Tuesday, 26 January 1909, the sharp frosts had been joined by a heavy mist which later thickened into a dense fog. By Wednesday this shrouded the whole of London and Essex, reaching as far as the mouth of the River Thames. The Tottenham inquest was held at 10.30 a.m. in the Municipal Buildings in Tottenham before the coroner, Mr Forbes. It was opened and the jury sworn in. Mr W H Pennington, a survivor of the Balaclava charge in the Battle of the Crimea, was elected jury foreman. He and the other jurors filed into the adjoining mortuary to view the remains of PC Tyler and Ralph Joscelyne. The first task of any inquest is to identify the deceased and this is usually done at the earliest opportunity. The identification is normally performed by a close family member of the deceased, who is then invited to give a little background information about him or her. In this way, the family, who have had to sit quietly whilst everybody else has worked around them for the first few days after the death, has an opportunity to be heard, and if they are worrying about giving evidence or facing the media, to get the task behind them.

Next to give evidence was Mr Joscelyne, who formally identified Ralph and recounted the events of the previous Saturday, which had culminated in his son's murder. The *Wood Green Herald* of 27 January 1909 stated that he gave his evidence in an indistinct voice and the report was accompanied by a photograph of him as he stood on the edge of the pavement outside the coroner's court. Unsurprisingly, he was reported to be rigid with grief.

By the time that the inquest had been adjourned until February, Helfeld had been committed for trial by coroner's warrant on a charge of murder. Later the same day, at 4 p.m., the Walthamstow coroner, Dr Ambrose, opened the inquest into the death of Jacob Lepidus, known at this time as Jacob (this was only three days after the incident and Paul Helfeld was still in hospital and expected to make a full recovery). A large crowd had gathered outside the court long before the time of the enquiry and when the court opened there was a rush to gain admission.

The first witness was Stanislaus Kolenski of Ashley Road, Tottenham. A Russian with a poor command of the English language, he had difficulties understanding and answering the questions put to him. He confirmed Jacob's identity, having seen the body in the mortuary, and stated that Jacob came from Riga, the capital of Latvia. Mr Kolenski also told the court that Jacob had once worked at Lebus' Timber Yard and rented a room from him from December 1907 to March 1908, when he threw him out. The coroner asked Mr Kolenski if he had evicted Jacob because he was penniless. Mr Kolenski replied: "Yes—he was no good to anybody. No money, no work, no pay." At this, there was laughter in the court.

Other witnesses, including the police involved in Jacob's shooting, gave their evidence. Among these was PC Eagles, who at this time was still convinced that it was *his* gun that had fired the fatal shot. The police surgeon, Dr Alcock, however, told the court that the bullet that he had retrieved from Jacob's skull after his death was the of same calibre and type as the one that remained in Jacob's own revolver when he was found. The bullets fired by PC Eagles were of a different calibre and type. The jury were allowed to examine the bullets before retiring. Within half an hour they had returned and the foreman pronounced a verdict of *felo de se,* indicating that Lepidus had died by his own hand. *Felo de se* is Latin for "felon of himself," an archaic legal term meaning suicide. Early English common law considered suicide a crime and a person found guilty of it, even though dead, was subject to punishments including forfeiture of property to the monarch and being given a shameful burial. Beginning in the 17th-century, law and custom gradually changed so as to regard a person who committed suicide to be temporarily insane (which was frequently reflected in the use of the term "whilst the balance of his or her mind was disturbed") at the time and conviction and punishment were gradually phased out, with persons attempting suicide being charged up to the 1950s and 1960s.

It was agreed that Jacob would be buried on the same day as PC Tyler and Ralph Joscelyne were to be interred at Abney Park Cemetery. Founded in 1840, Abney Park Cemetery is at South Lodge, Abney Park, Stoke Newington High St, London, in the London Borough of Hackney and is one of the "Magnificent Seven" garden cemeteries of London and a woodland memorial park and local nature reserve. The inquest was then adjourned.

The *Wood Green Herald* of 27 January 1909 reported that Helfeld was making good progress but that he was being watched closely. The newspaper printed a report from Mr Drewett, the resident governor of the Prince of Wales Hospital. "Even now", Mr Drewett was quoted as saying, "he is perfectly conscious and is constantly trying to get out of bed. He glares all around the ward with an expression of terrible ferocity, as if it maddens him to think of his impotence. He is a big fellow of a magnificent physique, very heavily developed. As he lies in bed, guarded on each side by a big policeman, he looks the dangerous ruffian he has shown himself to be. He has tried so often to get up — all through the night he kept thrusting his leg from under the clothes and trailing it along the floor — that it has been found necessary to fix a strong screen of boards around his bed."

The above comment that, "He looks the dangerous ruffian he has shown himself to be" sounds a little judgemental and impolitic today. It is difficult to believe that a hospital administrator nowadays would describe a patient as a "dangerous ruffian" and use the words "he has shown himself to be" — presumably by killing a policemen and a child, crimes which at that time he had yet to be even charged with.

The police kept an armed guard inside and outside of the hospital. Helfeld's presence caused considerable nervous tension to all the hospital staff, especially to the doctors and nurses who attended him. All the time that this was going on Scotland Yard had officers investigating the robbers' backgrounds. They discovered that Helfeld was wanted by the Russian police and that he was believed to have been involved in bank robberies in Scotland. They also learned that he had worked as a fireman on a Russian ship that plied the route between the Baltic ports and England, possibly as a way to distribute his propaganda and deliver firearms to his compatriots. They took Lepidus' fingerprints at the mortuary to assist them in their enquiries and later discovered that he too was a member of a notorious Russian family of revolutionaries and that he had been in England for four years, although not necessarily continuously. The *Wood Green Herald* of 29 January 1909 gave credence to this story. It also carried an article from a reporter on *The Star* newspaper, part of which read:-

> "One man who had been to the mortuary and seen Jacob's (Lepidus') corpse said to me:—'You will never get his proper name in this country. He has been identified with our movement for about four years and we never know each other's proper names. He was connected when he came over here with the Communist Club in Charlotte Street, Fitzroy Square. He was a member of the Boskeviky and merely joined to cloak acts of robbery such as this, which take place every day in Russia. He was a Lithuanian and as far as I know his family lived in the forests at the back of Riga.'"

The newspapers were keen to obtain an interview with Helfeld, and one enterprising reporter, Johann Nideroest, tried to gain admission to the Prince of Wales Hospital by posing as Helfeld's brother on the Monday evening after The Outrage, 25 January 1909.

At a special sitting of Tottenham Police Court on the evening of 27 January 1909, Chief Inspector John McCarthy, also of Scotland Yard, claimed to the court that Nideroest was "a sort of journalist of the sensational kind" and that his sole object in trying to see Helfeld was to obtain an interview to sell to the newspapers. Nideroest was discharged. The *Wood Green Herald* of 29 January 1909 also reported that police guarding Helfeld had been suspicious of his visitor, despite his giving an elaborate background history of his relationship with his "brother" Paul. Inspector Hester of Scotland Yard had been called to the hospital, where he recognised Nideroest as being connected with various secret societies in the East End of London.

The Funerals

In the week after The Outrage leading up to the funerals, the weather deteriorated. By Wednesday, heavy frost covered the capital and this, together with the dense, smoky and tenacious fog had brought life to a standstill. There were frequent road traffic accidents. At night, when people were attempting to return home from work, the terrible conditions made road and rail travel chaotic. Flares were set up at important traffic junctions and cab drivers had to get off their cabs and lead their horses on foot. On Thursday, the freezing fog continued and the highest recorded temperature was 28 degrees Fahrenheit, still below freezing. Despite the bad weather, advertisements appeared in *The Times* stating that as the ice at Hyde Water on the Welsh Harp at Hendon was in such splendid condition, skating races would take place on Friday, 29 January 1909 at 2 p.m.: the same date and time as the funerals of PC Tyler and Ralph Joscelyne.

By mid-day Friday the weather brightened and the temperature rose from below freezing to 44 degrees Fahrenheit. Despite the unpromising start to the day, the police had cleared the streets to allow for the thousands of spectators who were gathering from all over London to see the funeral cortege. So great was the throng that all traffic had to be diverted.

By order of Superintendent Jenkins, police officers were posted to the major railway stations in Tottenham, Seven Sisters, Bruce Grove and South Tottenham in order to direct sightseers to places where the least congestion was expected. Police from various forces, many of whom had sacrificed their rest day to attend, lined the route, where, long before the time of the funeral, crowds stood six deep on the pavements. Many others watched from upstairs windows, roofs and balconies. Hawkers did a brisk business in the sale of memorial cards bearing portraits of the two victims but, in view of the solemnity of the occasion, lowered their voices while touting their wares.

The *Daily Graphic* described the scene:

> "[T]he work of selling the cards gave employment to many who were obviously of the unemployed class. Indeed the presence of this class, and of a great army of loafers as well, was very marked all along the route. But the crowd was composed of all classes—women and men, old and young, the well-dressed, the shabbily-dressed and the ragged."

The *Daily Mirror* estimated that 500,000 people lined the route, and that 3,000 police officers had lined the one-and-a-half mile route from the Tyler family home in Arnold Road to Abney Park Cemetery, three deep. Only in the riots in 1985 and 2011 have there ever been more policemen on the streets of Tottenham! The lengthy procession was made up of:

- Black-plumed horses drawing PC William Tyler's coffin, which was draped in a Union Flag;
- White-plumed horses drawing Ralph Joscelyne's coffin;
- The Tyler Family
- The Joscelyne Family
- Representatives of the MPS (mounted and on foot);
- The MPS band;
- Representatives of the local fire brigade;
- Representatives of the Scots Guards;
- Representatives of Royal Garrison Artillery;
- Representatives of the local tramway company.

Ralph Joscelyne's mourners had gathered at his home. Mr Herbert Samuel MP, Under Secretary at the Home Department, representing the Home Secretary, and the MPS Commissioner, Sir Edward Henry, joined the procession at the Joscelyne Family home. They walked behind the hearse to Arnold Road where the smaller Joscelyne cortege joined the larger Tyler cortege. Despite the large crowd which had gathered in Arnold Road, the funeral procession left the Tyler family home at 2 p.m. sharp as arranged.

The *Daily Graphic* of 30 January had a reporter at the Tyler home, who described Mrs Tyler as "a pathetic figure upon whom every eye looked with sympathy as she walked to the mourning carriages". *Lloyds News* enlarged on this, stating that Mrs Tyler leaned heavily on the arm of her brother-in-law, while the *Daily Mirror* described her exclaiming in agonised tones: "Oh Lord, take me too." The grief of the Joscelyne family went unremarked.

The police band struck up the Dead March from Saul as the cortege left Arnold Road and traversed through the back streets to Tottenham High Road, stopping briefly outside the black-draped police station where the day duty policemen stood to attention paying a final tribute to their fellow officer. Many houses along the route had their blinds and curtains drawn, while all shops were closed, with black shutters erected as a sign of mourning. Flags at the municipal offices at High Cross and on other public buildings were flown at half-mast. The railway bridge at Stamford Hill was draped in black, and black crepe bows were attached to tramcars.

The procession was headed by a small detachment of mounted police inspectors. They were followed by the white-plumed hearse of Ralph Joscelyne, drawn by four white-plumed horses. Ralph's coffin was covered in wreaths, one of which came from his fellow pupils at Earlsmead School, and the hearse was escorted by a bodyguard of police officers on either side. Mr and Mrs Joscelyne and their family followed in three mourning coaches.

Immediately behind the Joscelyne cortege came a detachment of mounted police. PC Newman, who had been slightly wounded in the face by a bullet during the chase, was part of the next contingent of 12 constables and a sergeant, which formed the firing party. The band of "N" Division, playing dirges, preceded PC Tyler's hearse. The coffin, covered in a Union Flag, was borne in a black-plumed hearse by six black-plumed horses, the lead one being ridden by a black-clad postillion. On the coffin lay a floral emblem comprising a cushion, with his official number, 403 "N", worked in violets, on which rested PC Tyler's duty armband. Mrs Tyler's tribute, a harp with a broken string, also lay upon the coffin. Mrs Tyler, dressed in mourning black, carried a bouquet of white hothouse flowers sent by the Police Wives at Home and occupied the first of the six coaches allocated to PC Tyler's family and close friends. The senior Mrs Tyler, PC Tyler's stepmother, his four brothers, sister and half-sister were in the following coaches. Also in the family party was PC Tyler's niece, Mabel and her mother.

Behind these walked Herbert Samuel, Sir Edward Henry, the MPS commissioner and his assistant commissioners; these were followed by 200 men of "N" Division under the command of Superintendent Jenkins. Pall bearers from the force walked on either side of the hearse. Two glass-panelled carriages filled with wreaths followed.

The mourners also included the Tottenham and Edmonton Fire Brigade engine and firemen, detachments from the Scots Guards and the Royal Garrison Artillery, postmen and employees from both the Metropolitan and London County Council Tramway companies. Representatives of the West Ham and Hackney unemployed also marched. These were followed by police from all over London accompanied by massed bands. As the cortege passed, men in the silent crowds removed their hats as a sign of respect. The procession's journey took it past the Prince of Wales Hospital where Helfeld lay. Possibly he heard the dirges for those he had slain.

The procession was one-and-a-half miles long and took 25 minutes to pass any given spot. Despite leaving the Tyler home on time at two p.m. the cortege had taken twice the estimated time to arrive at the gates of Abney Park Cemetery and finally arrived at 4 p.m. instead of 3 p.m. As it did so a thick mist descended and dusk began to fall.

Two colour sergeants representing the 1st Battalion of the Scots Guards, two representatives of the Salvation Army and Mr Hyde, Secretary of the Benevolent and Visiting Committee of the PSA (Pleasant Sunday Afternoon) Brotherhood, Congregational Church, Enfield Highway were waiting at the gates, together with a deputation from the Hackney unemployed.

The procession was not allowed into the cemetery nor were members of the general public: police on duty kept back the crowds thronging the gates. There were scuffles and several women fainted in the crush. When the main cortege arrived at the chapel, the two coffins were carried in and placed upon biers in front of the reading-desk, while the organist played the Dead March. At this, Mrs Tyler burst into inconsolable sobbing. PC Tyler's coffin was carried by six of his fellow officers, while four policemen bore Ralph Joscelyne's. Both services were conducted by the chaplain, the Reverend A O Palmer. After his address, the organist of St Mary's, Stoke Newington played "O Rest Unto the Lord" and "I Know that My Redeemer liveth." The chaplain then concluded the brief service with the words from Matthew Chapter 25, verses 21–23: "Well done, thou good and faithful servant. Enter thou into the joy of thy Lord." As PC Tyler's coffin was carried from the chapel, Mrs Tyler broke down again, weeping violently. Her wild grief prompted many of the mourners to tears as well.

Amid the gathering gloom, the funeral parties walked to the gravesides. Both bodies were interred near the memorial to Dr Isaac Watts. That of Ralph Joscelyne was buried first. Amongst the wreaths was one from the police bearing the inscription: "From the Officers of Edmonton Station as a token of respect for the boy and his parents." The Church of England Service was carried out at the boy's grave without incident. During PC Tyler's burial, his widow's sobbing was continuous.

The hymn, *O God our Help in Ages Past*, having been sung, the band concluded with *Lead Kindly Light* which was accompanied by mourners singing at the gravesides. The police, division by division, filed bareheaded and slowly past the grave, with many weeping. A volley fired by the artillerymen indicated to the waiting crowds outside that the funerary rites were concluded. Mrs Tyler, accompanied by the Tyler and Joscelyne families, left the cemetery by the Church Street entrance together with the other mourners.

As the gates Abney Park Cemetery shut, those of Queen's Road Cemetery in Walthamstow opened and a solitary policeman kept guard. At the stroke of five o'clock, as the district council hooter sounded, the body of Jacob Lepidus, enclosed in a plain elm shell, which bore a plate inscribed "Jacob. Died 23 January 1909, aged about 30," left the mortuary, borne on the shoulders of four of the parish undertaker's men. The undertaker himself walked beside the coffin accompanied by the Reverend Robert Eastly, Baptist Minister of Walthamstow, who had been prevailed upon to bury the body, two police officers and the cemetery superintendent, Mr J Smith. Also present was a reporter from the *Kingsland & Hackney Gazette*. Slowly, in the descending blackness, the small party made its way to the extreme end of the cemetery where they halted before a newly dug grave in unconsecrated ground. The shell was lowered from the men's shoulders onto ropes held by two gravediggers and then passed from sight into darkness.

The minister, in ordinary clerical garb, went to the edge of the grave and said: "Inasmuch as it pleases God to take unto himself the soul of our brother, we therefore commit his body to the ground." He waited while the undertakers gathered a handful of earth, then continued: "Earth to earth, ashes to ashes, dust to dust."

Many of the small funeral party departed before he finished speaking, leaving only the gravediggers. Before they had filled in the grave, rain began to fall, and continued throughout the night, turning the freshly dug ground to mud. The reporter from the *Kingsland & Hackney Gazette*, writing on 30 January 1909, said that:

> "The gloom overhead had increased considerably since the little party had left the mortuary and rain now began to fall. Soon the diggers had finished their labours and so ended in fitting darkness the earthly career of this desperate man. There are no means save perhaps the freshly turned earth whereby the grave can be identified. The funeral expenses will be borne by the West Ham Guardians."

Half a million local people showed their respect and appreciation for PC Tyler's sacrifice and their opposition to foreign terrorists attacking their country and its institutions by also lining the route. Only members of the Royal Family and a few Prime Ministers are recognised in this way. Never before had there been such a widespread demonstration of public sorrow at a police officer's funeral. The blinds of all the houses on the route had been closely drawn and shops were closed for the day with black shutters put up as a sign of mourning. Flags were lowered to half-mast and mourning cards were sold to members of the public.

The front page of the *Daily Mirror* on Saturday 30 January 1909 is shown below:

Pictured from left are: Sir Edward Henry — Commissioner
of the MPS and H Samuel, Under Secretary at the
Home Office. Right the funeral procession

On Monday 1 February 1909, Baron Alphonse Heyking, the consul general at the Imperial Russian Consulate in London, wrote to the commissioner to say that he was sending a wreath and asking that it be placed on PC Tyler's grave to show his "admiration for the [MPS], to which the deceased belonged." There was no mention of young Ralph, the other victim of the robbery. At the end of his letter the baron made the point that: "The murderer who is said to be a Russian subject was not a Russian speaking ethnographically." Apparently, the Russians had no problems in invading or conquering Latvia, but they saw no need to take responsibility for the actions of those of their citizens who were not ethnically pure Russians.

Anarchist groups across Europe were quick to portray Helfeld and Lepidus as heroes.

"Last week the dailies related in detail a tragic incident of the social struggle. In the suburbs of London (in Tottenham) two of our Russian comrades attacked the accountant [he was the office-boy] of a factory and, pursued by the crowd and the police, held out in a desperate struggle, the mere recounting of which is enough to make one shiver...After almost two hours of resistance, having exhausted their munitions, and wounded 22 people, three of them mortally [it was two], they reserved for themselves their final bullets...We today insist on saying loudly and clearly: The London 'bandits' were at one with us!...I can guess, dear reader, the sentimental objection that is on your lips: But the 22 unfortunates wounded by your comrades' bullets were innocent! Have you no remorse? No! For those who pursued them could have been nothing but 'honest' citizens, believers in the state, in authority. Perhaps oppressed, but oppressed who, by their criminal weakness, perpetuate oppression. Enemies!" (*Le Révolté*, a journal published in Geneva)

For some reason the article failed to point out that one of the enemies the poor downtrodden "Russian Comrades" had faced was a ten-year-old boy. Fortunately, Ralph's mother, Louise Joscelyne did not see that article.

Ralph's father died shortly after his murder, of a broken heart according to the family. His mother, Louise Joscelyne never remarried and lived on until 1952 when she still had the pair of small boots worn by her son when he died. They had been returned to her from the mortuary after the post-mortem and she kept them highly polished. Her last request was that they be buried with her and after a final shine they were placed carefully in her coffin.

Helfeld's Death in Hospital

Away from the public gaze, Paul Helfeld remained in hospital under police guard. No indication had been given of the date when he would appear at the magistrates' court for committal proceedings to the Assizes.

While he had initially made good progress, on 9 February 1909 a further operation was carried out to remove pieces of bone from the entrance to the head wound which had caused compression of the brain and meningitis. He did not recover and died on February 12 from meningitis and shock. His funeral took place on 18 February and was attended by a reporter from the *Wood Green Herald* who wrote that "Paul Helfeld, died 12 February 1909, aged 21 years":

"Such was the inscription on the tin plate that surmounted an elm coffin that contained the remains of the wretched assassin, which was lowered into the grave at an out of the way un-consecrated portion of Tottenham Cemetery yesterday morning soon after ten o'clock. The body was removed from the mortuary at Clyde Road Council Depot and passing out of the back way into Clyde Road, only two or three officials were aware of what was going on. When it arrived at the cemetery, the body was quickly borne to the grave. Inspector Gould, the undertakers' men, the gravedigger and reporters were the only witnesses."

Like his accomplice Lepidus, Helfeld's passing was unwept, unhonoured and unsung. It was subsequently reported that Helfeld's only words while in hospital were: "My mother is in Riga". The Burial Register for Tottenham Cemetery records: "Paul Helfeld — buried 18 February 1909 aged 21 — grave general 6442." A pauper's grave.

The stories about Latvian Activists in 1909 and 1911 attracted considerable media coverage. When the news of The Outrage and the Siege of Sidney Street featured on *Pathé News* at local cinemas, which were popular at the time, Winston Churchill, the Home Secretary, was jeered and people called for him to be shot for failing to strictly enforce the Aliens Act. This criticism caused Churchill to strengthen the legislation, and he proposed the Aliens (Prevention of Crime) Bill under the ten minute rule. Another MP, Josiah C Wedgwood, a descendant of the Staffordshire ceramics entrepreneur, objected and wrote to Churchill to ask him not to introduce the hard-line measures: "You know as well as I do that human life does not matter a rap in comparison with the death of ideas and the betrayal of English traditions." The bill did not become law.

Today Abney Park Cemetery is a nature reserve. Trees and bushes cover much of the ground. The chapel where the burial services for PC Tyler and Ralph Joscelyne were held is now derelict and a memorial to the local dead of the two world wars overshadows their tombs. Throughout the cemetery and along the path now named for PC Tyler, many gravestones are hidden under the lush undergrowth, but his remains clear. Beneath a canopy at the top of this distinctive monument, which bears PC Tyler's number — 403 — stands an urn. Upon the urn lies a folded cape surmounted by a police helmet. This stone carving, with supporting pillars and canopy stand upon a base of red marble, fronted by a matching kerb. Behind this, not far away from PC Tyler's grave, lies the simpler memorial to Ralph Joscelyne. For decades Ralph's grave was overlooked and neglected, until being re-discovered in the 1980s by a group of schoolchildren from the school that Ralph attended, Earlsmead School who as this book went to press were doing a project on The Outrage.

PC Zeithing died at sea on active service in 1916 and in 1919 Superintendent Jenkins died, shortly after his retirement.

What Did Happen to the Stolen Money?

The subject of the stolen money occupied many peoples' minds. The indefatigable *Wood Green Herald* reported that apart from the five pounds found on Jacob, no sign of the remaining 75 pounds had been discovered. So what did happen to the proceeds? This was the entire purpose of the day, so where did it all go? The two Latvians had risked, and eventually lost, their lives to get their hands on the money, so they would not easily have given it up. It was gold, silver and bronze coin in a black wages bag, which had not been seen since it was snatched from the wages clerk. The two robbers would have needed both hands to wrestle the two men who had delivered the money to the factory onto the ground, but they could perhaps have picked up the bag before they ran off. If not, perhaps another person had had the presence of mind to discretely pick it up and quietly put it somewhere safe where he or she could collect it later?

The chase was conducted at speed, and the robbers fired off a shot on average every 20 seconds, so they would have needed both their hands to push people and objects out of the way, to assist them to leap over obstacles and to hold their guns. Eighty pounds in coin would have weighed a little over 22 pounds/ten kilogramme. You would not enter a ten kilometre road race wearing a heavy over coat and boots and loaded down with that sort of weight in your pockets, but that is what the Latvians did.

The *Wood Green Herald* reported that five pounds was found on Lepidus' body, but that no money at all had been found on Helfeld's, so that if the five pounds from Lepidus was from the proceeds of the robbery, then the other 75 pounds was still missing.

Subsequent commentators have suggested variously that the robbers might have had an accomplice who discreetly collected the bag from them during the chase, that the bag was left in the bushes to be picked up later and was found by another thief, that the bag was dumped in the river as they crossed it planning to return later to collect it, or that Lepidus pushed it up the chimney in Oak Cottage when he was finally cornered there.

The police must have been asking the same question. If there was an accomplice, then he was gone. The police checked the robber's backgrounds for the coroner, but no accomplice was discovered. No doubt police officers were sent to re-trace the route of the chase and to speak to local residents to collect up any useful exhibits from the event, but no trace was ever reported of the bag. The police emptied the River Lea between Picketts Lock and Stonebridge Lock, and searched the river bed without success.

Many years later, local gossip was that the Rolstone family was living well beyond its means. The suspicion was that they found the money up the chimney and said nothing. The family ignored the gossip and kept tight-lipped. Many more years passed before Charles Rolstone junior, the young boy who had been trapped in Oak Cottage by Lepidus at the end of the chase, gave an interview to local historian, Ray Dudley of Whipps Cross Hospital Radio and the Tape Recorders Guild and admitted that Oak Cottage partially collapsed during a storm several years after the incident and that, while clearing the rubble afterwards, a sum of money was found in what was left of the fireplace in the front parlour. He did not disclose exactly when this happened or precisely how much money.

But perhaps this was why Lepidus had climbed up the chimney just before he went upstairs and put his pistol to his head and killed himself?

Commemorative poster.

CHAPTER 10

Awards, Recognition and Words of Appreciation

As might be expected with an incident that had attracted so much media and public attention, it did not take long for awards to be made to a number of both police and citizens involved in the incident.

On 23 March 1909, Police Orders announced that five constables were to be promoted to the rank of sergeant without the usual requirement for them to pass the qualifying examination: "Being of sufficiently long service to be eligible for this rank." These officers were:

- Police Constable Cater;
- Police Constable Dewhurst;
- Police Constable Dixon;
- Police Constable Eagles;
- Police Constable Nicod.

PC Eagles, DC Eagles and PC Cater were the three officers who had ascended the stairs in Oak Cottage and confronted Jacob Lepidus so that he committed suicide.

PC Nicod was the most seriously injured of all the police officers.

PC Dewhurst had, with Mr Charles Schaffer, rescued the Rolstone children from Oak Cottage when Lepidus was in there preparing to confront the police.

The same Police Order also recognised the contributions of PC's Newman and Zeithing, but noted that they were young in service (and presumably not therefore "[Of] sufficiently long service to be eligible for this rank") so that instead they were advanced to the highest rate of pay for their existing rank.

PC Newman had taken a strong lead at the scene of the robbery and witnessed his colleague, PC Tyler being shot and killed.

PC Zeithing had three shots fired at him and, despite this, continued the pursuit.

The only other people who had been at Oak Cottage and played a significant role in ending the chase were Inspector Gould and Station Police Sergeant Hart, who had managed the incident and the two civilians, Thomas Brown, who had actually joined the three officers in ascending the stairs to confront Lepidus, and Charles Schaffer, who had been with PC Dewhurst in Oak Cottage when he rescued the Rolstone children. Of course, Mrs Tyler may well have considered that he husband having been killed whilst pursuing the robbers, deserved posthumous recognition.

The Home Secretary, Mr Herbert Gladstone, sent a letter to Sir Edward Henry, the commissioner of the MPS, from which an extract was published in the same Police Orders.

"These officers faced imminent danger without hesitation and their promptitude and gallantry...richly deserves this recognition".

These officers also received awards of various sums from the Bow Street Fund and medallions from the Carnegie Hero Fund Trust.

Later the commissioner made awards of £1 to six officers. This does not sound much, but allowing for inflation it was the equivalent today of £110 and it should be remembered that the men working at Schnurmann's Rubber Factory were due to receive an average weekly pay package of just half of a pound (ten shillings: 10/-) for a week's work.

- PS 44 "N" Mackay
- PS 67 "N" Jowett
- PC 755 "N" Lawrence
- PC 807 "N" Willison
- PC 637 "N" Frasier; and
- PC 222 "J" Bleadon.

Interestingly, none of these officers' names appear elsewhere in this book, except for PC Frasier who was one of the officers who leapt out of the station window, and who was present at the scene of the robbery. It is also possible that PS Jowett is the same person as PS Howett, who was shot at by the robbers at Hagger Bridge. Perhaps their absence from the book, shows the great depth of the chase and that only a small proportion of the brave deeds that occurred are publicly known.

The commissioner also made "Notes in Favour" of 12 officers:

Chief Inspector Holland

Divisional Detective Insp Martin

Sub Divisional Inspector Haines

PS (CID) Haigh

PC 236 "N" Adams

PC 288 "N" Baldwin

PC 853 "N" Brewer

PC 334 "N" Brown

PC 153 "N" Commerford

PC 616 "N" Francis

PC 747 "N" Shakespeare

PC 442 "J" Wilson.

PCs Adams, Francis and Shakespeare had been prominent with PS Jowett at Hagger Bridge, and PC Shakespeare is the officer who took possession of Helfeld's gun when he killed himself, but none of the other officers appear in our story.

Many other officers received commendations written on vellum.

The day after the Police Order, 24 March 1909 at Bow Street Magistrates' Court, cheques in the amounts shown were awarded to the following officers from the Carnegie Hero Fund Trust:

- Inspector Gould (£15, equivalent to around £1,650 today);
- PS Hale £12.10.0 (equivalent to £1,375 today);
- PS Hart £12.10.0 (as above);
- PC Bond £10 (equivalent to £1,100 today);
- PC Field £10 (as above);
- PC Rushbrooke £10 (as above);
- PC Spedding £10 (as above).

Inspector Gould had, with PS Hale attempted to stop the robbers crossing into The Marshes. He had also taken control of the conclusion of the chase at Oak Cottage.

PS Hale had, with Inspector Gould, attempted to stop the robbers crossing into The Marshes. He also commandeered the car at Hagger Bridge.

SPS Hart had also taken control of the conclusion of the chase at Oak Cottage.

PC Bond had, with PC Frasier, jumped out of the police station window at the start of the robbery.

PC Spedding had fired four shots at the robbers at Banbury Reservoir, just after they had shot Sidney Slater. The interesting question is what he would have received if his two shots had killed the two robbers and ended the pursuit.

PCs Field and Rushbrook do not appear in this story.

Superintendent Jenkins, the officer in charge of the Stoke Newington Division, which at that time included Tottenham, who had written the closing report on the incident which is printed in full at *Appendix 1* to this volume, received an "appreciation of excellent services rendered" from the Home Secretary. The commissioner, at a Board of Inquiry into The Outrage, praised Superintendent Jenkins "for the prompt and diligent manner in which they [the police] were distributed" and presented him with a silver-plated tea and coffee set. Many officers who have faced terrorists armed with semi-automatic weapons question why a particular officer was selected for senior rank. If it was for his excellent report writing then why should he or she be commended when he or she does the job that they are paid to do? Jenkins never even made it to the front of the chase.

In his report, Jenkins makes special mention of the police officers working inside the police station:

"Station Police Sergeant Jones was in charge of Tottenham Police Station at the time of The Outrage. He rendered very good service and so many were the enquiries that he was kept talking almost continually for the whole period, causing temporary inflammation and swelling of the throat which continued for two days but he did not go sick. As to the clerical staff, I mention them because of the excessive work entailed by this enquiry, necessitating long hours and on two occasions night and day continuously, except for a short break of about three hours". (MEP03/194)

Another senior officer, Sub-Divisional Inspector Large, who with PC Newman, had carried PC Nathan to safety after he had been shot, called an ambulance for him and comforted him whilst they waited for it to arrive, also received an "appreciation of excellent services rendered" from the Home Secretary. What else was he supposed to do, abandon a dying officer?

Of course, these were the days was class really mattered. I am reminded that my grandfather won a Military Medal and was commissioned in the field at the Battle of the Somme in the First World War, just six years after this incident. He did not receive the Military Cross, for which the criteria were the same, because that was reserved for officers only. When he got home he found a letter from his work. It was addressed, "Dear Barton" not "Dear Mr Barton", because he was only an employee. The letter congratulated him on his award and on his brave deeds and was signed by 22 of the directors of the company "Smith, Jones, Bloggs, etc., etc. ..."

On 17 July 1909, as a direct consequence of The Outrage, the King announced that he had decided to create a new medal to show his appreciation for police officers shown to have displayed exceptional bravery or service. It would be called the Kings Police Medal (KPM). Of course, when a woman is on the throne it is called the Queen's Police Medal (QPM). On 9 November 1909 it was announced that the new medal was being awarded to three newly promoted police sergeants, Eagles, Dixon and Cater, the three officers who were at Oak Cottage and who had cornered Lepidus, so that he appears to have felt that he had no alternative but to commit suicide. On the morning of 2 July 1910 the medals were presented to the officers by King Edward VII at a private ceremony held at Marlborough House.

Unfortunately, at the time of its creation, the KPM was only awarded to living people, so PC Tyler still did not receive an award. Today the medal is also awarded posthumously to officers.

The names of another 70 police officers, whose conduct appeared to merit special consideration, had their names passed to the "Tottenham Outrage Fund" for an award.

And the Civilian Heroes?

At the Tottenham Inquest into the deaths of PC Tyler and Ralph Joscelyne, the coroner had remarked that the gas stoker, Mr George Smith, who had run to assist the victims of the robbery, had been "a plucky man and deserved great praise". At a special ceremony at Tottenham Council Chamber in March 1909, Smith received £25 (equivalent to £2,750 today) and an illustrated testimonial from his employers, the Hornsey Gas Company.

In May 1909, decisions were made on all the 32 applications for compensation that had been submitted to the police (including that of Superintendent Jenkins) and which are further discussed in *Chapter 8* and set out in *Appendix 9*.

The sum of £30 was awarded to the Prince of Wales Hospital in Tottenham and £15 to Walthamstow Hospital, which had between them cared for most of the wounded. Letters of thanks were sent to both establishments.

Frederick Mortimer was awarded £100;

William Roker was awarded £50;

Mrs Joscelyne was awarded £10;

Emily Tyler was awarded £8;

Charles Schaffer, was awarded £2;

Mrs Mary Ann Cawley was awarded £1.

Mr Mortimer and Mr Roker had been wounded when they were shot by the robbers.

Mrs Joscelyne had lost her son and Emily Tyler had lost her husband.

Charles Schaffer had put his life at risk by entering Oak Cottage with PC Dewhurst to rescue the Rolstone children. Dewhurst had been promoted to sergeant and Schaffer, although not eligible for promotion, must have been a little disappointed to receive only £2, especially when Mary Ann Cawley was awarded £1 for throwing a potato at the robbers.

The amounts are unusual and it would be interesting to know how they were calculated. Young Ralph was a ten-year-old schoolboy and no doubt, a drain on his family's finances. PC Tyler was the breadwinner for his family. So why did Mrs Joscelyne get more than Mrs Tyler?

Emily Tyler, having lost her husband whilst he was in the course of his duty as a police officer, qualified for a pension from the MPS. There was a short delay whilst the sum to be paid was calculated and she did not receive the first payment until 14 June 1909, five months after her husband's murder. No doubt his pay had been stopped far more quickly, so that she had had to rely on any savings, borrow from relatives, and make cutbacks in order to pay the rent and feed the family.

The amount of any pension to be paid to a police officer or his widow is clearly set down in Police Regulations and in this case was determined to be £15 per annum. The regulations also set down that should the police widow re-marry, then the entire pension would be forfeited immediately. Presumably, when Mrs Tyler married PC William George Williams of "J" Division on 15 April 1915 at the St James the Less Church in Bethnal Green, she ceased to receive her police pension in respect of PC Tyler.

A pension of £15 meant that Mrs Tyler would have 5/9d (29 pence) per week to live on. To put this in context, it was discussed earlier in this book that Schnurmann's Rubber Factory paid the lowest wages in town, so that no British person would work for them and they were forced to employ immigrants (often supplying false names). Yet their average salary of 10/0d (50 pence) was almost double what Mrs Tyler was receiving. Was she being "forced" to go out and look for a new husband? Was the pressure that she felt the reason that she entered what transpired to be an unsuitable marriage to PC Williams? When Williams committed suicide in 1924 did the former Mrs Tyler get another pension, or did she miss out completely?

The issue of Mrs Tyler's police pension raised considerable debate in the *Police Review* of 5 February 1909. Contributors pointed out that if PC Tyler had died of natural causes whilst in police employment she would have been treated far more generously and would not have lost her police pension if she had re-married.

A fund was established to receive public contributions for Mrs Tyler. At the recommendation of the Prime Minister, Herbert Gladstone, the King arranged to make a contribution of £100 to the fund from the Royal Bounty Fund. Gladstone personally donated £10 to the collection, while several other notable people gave £25 each. At Gladstone's request the King arranged for a payment of £100 to Mrs Tyler from the Royal Bounty Fund.

On 2 February 1909 the *Kingsland & Hackney Gazette* reported that on the day of the funerals £100 had been sent to the Widow's Fund as a result of a collection of one shilling (5p) per head on the floor of the Stock Exchange. On 10 February 1909, the *Wood Green Herald* reported that professional footballers at Tottenham Hotspur (Spurs) had collected £2.12.6 for Mrs Tyler and the parents of Ralph Joscelyne. During a match between Spurs and Hull City, the Tottenham Town Band had collected £5.11.0. Money poured in from subscribers, including the police in Wiltshire and Cornwall, plus a subscription from Leicestershire police who had raised £30.4s 4d. Other sums as small as 6d or as large as £25 were received from the public. All donations were forwarded to the Bow Street Magistrates' Court Fund.

On 5 February 1909 the *Police Review* reported that Sir Albert de Rutzen of Bow Street Police Court had informed the press that the fund had been closed with "sufficient money to meet the case's requirements". Whether this was a purely arbitrary personal decision or whether he had consulted Mrs Tyler in making it, is unclear. The fund had raised £1,055, but none of this would be given to Mrs Tyler herself. Instead, it was placed in the hands of the Public Trustees and she would receive the interest payable on the amount for her lifetime and at the time of her death the principal would be paid to the Metropolitan and City Police Orphanage.

Memorial Services

A number of memorial services were held for those who died during The Outrage. On 31 January 1909 a memorial service, which Mrs Emily Tyler attended, was held at the Salvation Army Citadel in Tottenham. The *Wood Green Herald* published a note of thanks from Mrs Tyler to Madam Vaughan of 10 Grand Parade, Green Lanes, Haringey, who had provided her mourning clothes free of charge.

On the afternoon of 18 July 1909 a memorial service for PC Tyler was held at All Saints' Church, Childs Hill, where he had attended and participated in the church choir as a boy. During the service a bronze plaque was unveiled commemorating his murder. On 23 July 1909 the *Hendon & Finchley Times* reported that Mrs Tyler had been amongst those in attendance at the service, together with other members of PC Tyler's family. Also present were PC Tyler's old choirmaster, Mr E. Sharpe and Superintendent Jenkins. The church was crowded, with many of those attending unable to obtain seats.

The Police Band played Handel's "Largo," and PCs Stiwell and Hames performed solos on the cornet and euphonium respectively. Seven Carnegie medallists, newly-promoted PS's Eagles, Nicod, Dewhurst, Cater and Detective Sergeant Dixon and PCs Zeithing and Newman, were in the unveiling procession for the plaque and the unveiling was performed out by Major Wodehouse, CB, assistant commissioner of the MPS. The newspaper reported that the plaque was designed by the Artificers Guild. Four saints are depicted: Michael, George, Martin and Maurice and columns of vine represent emblems of suffering and passion, while the laurel wreath surrounding the image of PC Tyler signifies victory.

The *Hendon Advertiser* of the same date described the text taken by the Reverend W D Petter, vicar of All Saints' from words on the memorial: "Be thou faithful unto death and I will give you a crown of life". The Reverend Petter concluded his address thus:

"Their [fellow police officers] object in attending the service was not to make a sensation, but as a reverent act of worship in memory of one who had been 'faithful unto death'."

More Media Coverage and Commemorations

In the weeks that followed The Outrage, a number of further stories were reported in the local press around Tottenham and Walthamstow:

On 29 January 1909, the *Daily Graphic* noted that Sir Edward Henry, the commissioner, had given his patronage to a mammoth carnival which would be held at the Empress Roller Skating Rink at Earls Court, on the following Friday, in aid of Mrs Tyler.

On 12 February 1909, the *Wood Green Herald* announced that a concert planned for the Palace Theatre in Tottenham High Road on Sunday 14 February 1909, in connection with the National Sunday League, would be for the benefit of sufferers from The Outrage, and the directors of the theatre had granted free use of the building. Among the attractions would be a speech by the local MP, Percy Alden.

On 19 February 1909, the *Wood Green Herald* reported that the Palace Theatre's managers had engaged for that week only the services of Captain Tupper — otherwise known as Harry Vaux. The article informed readers that Tupper, dressed in a policeman's uniform, sung an original song which mentioned PC Tyler, and that "the wording of the ditty had evoked a positive storm of applause." The proceeds would benefit sufferers from The Outrage.

On 29 January 1909, the *Hendon & Finchley Times* carried an account of PC Tyler's last visit to his family. This had occurred on the Sunday before his death when he had visited his stepmother, accompanied by his wife Emily, who had recently been discharged from the Prince of Wales Hospital after undergoing surgery. The family party had taken tea and discussed PC Tyler's work. Sobbing, PC Tyler's stepmother told the reporter she had not been expecting their visit and none of them imagined it would be the last time PC Tyler would enter that room.

On 12 February 1909, the *Wood Green Herald* published a message from Ralph Joscelyne's father. This said:

"Mr Joscelyne wishes to convey the heartfelt thanks of himself and Mrs Joscelyne to the general public for their sympathy and to Mr Seaward for giving their child such a splendid funeral free of cost. He also wishes to add a word of praise for the officers and men of the police whose generosity and kindness he will never forget."

On 23 January 2009, the centenary of The Outrage was marked by a number of events. A brown rectangular plaque was placed on the side of Tottenham Police Station in Chesnut Road. It reads,

"In memory of William Frederick Tyler, Police Constable 403 of 'N' Division, MPS, fallen while bravely serving the community on the 23rd January 1909."

A blue plaque was unveiled on the front of the Good Shepherd Church in Mitchley Road, Tottenham, where Ralph Joscelyne died. It reads,

"In memory of Ralph Joscelyne, 1899–1909 who was shot on this spot during the Tottenham Outrage on Jan 23rd 1909. May he rest in peace. *Justorum animae in manu dei sunt*"

The Latin translates as "The Souls of the righteous are in the hands of God".

A group of invited guests gathered at Tottenham Police Station. It was a cold, wet and blustery day and they were then taken by minibus to Abney Park Cemetery in Stoke Newington, to lay commemorative wreaths on the graves of the victims, PC William Tyler and Ralph Joscelyne.

Clearly the memory of the events and participants of The Outrage still live on...

CHAPTER 11

The Tottenham Outrage Today

It is now well over 100 years since the events recorded in this book. Even Ralph Joselyne, the schoolboy shot dead in the robbery would be 118-years-old if he was still alive. Nobody is still alive today who witnessed the events. There are, however, several historians who have met and spoken to all the main witnesses and recorded their testimony first-hand. Some have produced booklets of the event; some have travelled around telling the story to local groups in Tottenham and Walthamstow and on cruise ships; some have told the story online to an audience that had not even been conceived when these events took place.

The area around Tottenham and Walthamstow has changed dramatically. In 1909, they were separated by The Marshes, an area ten miles long and two miles wide, ranging from Enfield Lock in the north to the London 2012 Olympic Park in Stratford in the south, and from Tottenham in the west and Walthamstow in the east. In 1909, the area was occupied and controlled by children and adults rarely entered it. On the edges of The Marshes there was a rifle range and an area where people went duck shooting, a football pitch and Muslim Cemetery. Now the entire area has been drained and converted into housing and little evidence remains of The Marshes of old, although there are a number of rivers and railway lines crossing the area.

Outside The Marshes, the old streets and the old street names remain largely unchanged, but the buildings lining those streets have largely been demolished and replaced with new ones. Accordingly, the informal names given to areas by the local residents have disappeared. Considerable research was necessary to identify the location of Hagger Bridge in Forest Road, where the robbers had been confronted by police. Salisbury

Hall Farm has changed into Walthamstow Stadium, which in turn is changing into a modern housing estate. Kite's Corner, named after a famous shop, at the junction of Chingford Road and Farnan Road, has disappeared along with Kite's Shop.

Having walked the chase route I was most impressed by the level of the robbers' fitness. The route is only six-and-a-half miles long, but it would have been as strenuous as almost any marathon today, with the robbers wearing extremely thick, heavy woollen coats and jackets that would have restricted movement, weighed several pounds, and made running difficult, hot and sweaty. The majority of the route was through The Marshes, where the robbers would have sunk down in the mud until their knees and possibly their hips had disappeared into the mud and they would have had to pull their feet out after each step. In addition and so far as anyone can tell, the robbers were carrying the black canvas bag containing £21 in coins that they had stolen from the wages clerks. A great deal of the route is also uphill. Of course, the robbers by this time knew that they faced the death penalty having shot a ten-year-old boy and a policeman; they were not about to give themselves up to the police to face trial and he hangman.

The best section of the route to visit in order to get a feel for the area at the time of the robbery is the section from the Dust Destructor (now the council refuse depot) in Park View Road across the railway bridge at Down Lane Crossing at the end of Roseberry Avenue, into the final remains of The Marshes.

Memorials

There are five memorials to The Outrage, two of these on the route of the chase. One is on the side wall of Tottenham Police Station in Chesnut Road and the other is on the front wall of the church in Mitchley Road. The local residents are all familiar with the terms, "Tottenham Outrage" and "Walthamstow Tram Chase", although few have more than a casual knowledge of the incident. Local residents associations, historical societies, council and other archives and cruise companies are all interested in arranging presentations on it. The internet currently gives access to some 200 references to the event.

My contribution has been to use what I hope are the skills of a long-serving career detective to collect together all the available witnesses' accounts, examine statements, and combine these into one complete narrative, which is then placed in context and explained. I have used my knowledge and experience of the police and policing to explain why things were done in a certain way. By doing so I have been able to go back to my friend, Mike Waldren, and tell him the same story that he told me 36 six years ago when we were training to use firearms and which he has continued to investigate since that time, and expand the scope and pleasure that the story gives him.

I am aware that despite my careful efforts there may be discrepancies in this book and I am confident that, as always, my readers, with their eye for detail, will identify them. Witnesses stand in different places and always see things from a different angle and perspective. The only way to get witnesses to all tell the same story is to get them to lie and I would not do that. It is better to attempt to resolve their differences and I have tried to do this in this book and to justify each of my decisions. But I have also included copies of police reports and these cannot be changed today. Some were written in the hours after The Outrage when the facts were not fully-known or understood. The fact that the police reports confirm 99 per cent of the facts is pleasing.

Normally in a case like this, the police conduct an investigation, trace all the witnesses they can, take statements from them, and then collate these into a report which is submitted to the barrister conducting the case for the prosecution at court. After the trial, journalists and authors conduct another investigation into some of the more interesting and unusual aspects of the case and they often trace witnesses, take statements and collate them into a newspaper feature or book. After The Outrage, both suspects were dead and the police restricted their activities to a management report for the commissioner and the Home Secretary, and in dealing with the 32 claims for compensation. Several journalists and authors identified potential witnesses, traced and took statements from them, but collating the substantial number of statements into one coherent story was beyond them and each of the writers settled for reporting just a version of events from one witness — and several of these have indeed been circulated. Coming to the story 180 years after the incident, I have not been able to speak directly to witnesses, but I have, for the first time so I believe, fitted the pieces of the entire jig-saw together, collated the story and told it in all its glory. Several generations of readers have enjoyed aspects of the case; now, for the first-time, I hope that the current generation will enjoy having the benefit of reading the whole tragic story.

APPENDIX 1

Metropolitan Police Report[1]

Stoke Newington Station
"N" Division
7th day of February 1909

MURDER, ATTEMPTED MURDERS, SHOOTING AND THE ARREST OF THE MURDERERS BY POLICE. "N" DIVISION

I beg to report that at 10.30 a.m. 23rd ult [ultimo: last month] Joseph Wilson, a chauffeur, age 29, of 22 West Hampstead Mews, Hampstead accompanied by Albert Keyworth, age 17, an office boy, of 16 Seaford Road, South Tottenham, arrived at the factory of Schnurmann rubber merchant, Chesnut Road, Tottenham, in a motor car. The youth alighted carrying a canvas bag, containing about £80 [in] gold, silver and bronze, which he had had brought from the London and South Western Bank, South Hackney, for the wages of the men, a weekly custom.

Two men of foreign type, name[s] Jacob and Helfeld stood at the entrance of the premises, one at each side, Jacob seized the boy and bag and shot at him but inflicted no injury. There was a momentary struggle, they both fell but the man got up with the money. The chauffeur went promptly to the boy's assistance when he was seized by Jacob, he however laid hold of the bag and grasped Jacob by the throat, both fell and struggled desperately. Helfeld shot at the chauffeur repeatedly; his overcoat was riddled with bullets and a slanting shot passed through every garment, including his under vest, in the region of his stomach. Jacob released himself and discharged his revolver at him. In a miraculous and unaccountable way he

---

1. Source MPS/National Archives. All documentary appendices and charts are reproduced as originally written apart from minor, non-consequential or typographical changes.

escaped injury. The chauffeur cried loudly for help and a man name George Smith, a gas stoker, of 17 Hartington Road Tottenham went and gripped Jacob and threw him, the bag of money falling upon the pavement. Whilst struggling together Smith was shot in the chest by Helfeld, Jacob released himself and took the money at the same moment discharging his revolver at Smith. His escape from death was equally remarkable.

The assailants then ran off towards Tottenham marshes proceeding by way of Chesnut Grove, Scales Road and Mitchley Road.

The revolver shots were heard by Police at the Tottenham Police Station situated immediately opposite the rubber factory. PCs 403 "N" Tyler and 510 "N" Newman who were on reserve duty ran out. The chauffeur rapidly explained the position of things and with the latter PC got into the car and followed them. PC Tyler pursued on foot.

PC 406 "N" Bond and 637 "N" Fraiser, hearing the alarm, jumped through the open boot room window into Chesnut Road, followed by other officers who were aroused from sleep and who hastily put on some clothing and ran out by the front entrance and took up the chase.

The car overtook the assailants at Mitchley Road and the occupants were met by a fusillade of shots, damaging the glass wind screen, hood and radiator of the car, rendering it useless.

PC Newman received a graze on the cheek and a small wound on the lobe of his right ear. A crowd of persons joined in the chase, among them was Ralph Joscelyne aged 10 years a school boy of 3 Rugby House, Colsterworth Road, Tottenham, who was mortally wounded by a bullet wound in to his right breast. He was conveyed to the Tottenham Hospital where was found to be dead. He was subsequently identified by his mother.

After these incidents the murderers proceeded rapidly by way of the road to the Dust Destructor, situated on the marshes in a north-easterly direction. Constables Tyler and Newman crossed in a northerly direction with a view of heading them. When opposite the Dust Destructor Tyler was approaching them from the marsh land and called upon them to surrender but the man Helfeld, who is living, stood and took deliberate aim and shot him in the head which proved almost immediately fatal. Constable Newman remained with his fallen comrade. Sub Divisional Inspector Large arrived, Tyler was carried into a house nearby, an ambulance was sent for and he was conveyed with all speed to Tottenham Hospital and five minutes after admission died.

The chase which had now become most desperate was continued with a splendid determination. The murderers proceeded over the footbridge spanning the Great Eastern Railway, then in a north-easterly direction to the west bank of the River Lea. Following this course to Chalk Bridge which spans the river just beyond the rifle butts, thence onto the Mill Stream Bridge where they held the crowd at bay for a considerable time. It was here that PC 313 "N" Nicod went a short distance ahead of the crowd, knelt down upon the banks with a view of shooting the murderers, but the revolver, a private one which he had was found to be defective, before he could beat a retreat, both miscreants fired upon him and both shots took effect, he was wounded in the calf of his left leg and thigh and just previously a lad named Cyril Burgess of 63 Wycombe Road, Tottenham was wounded by a bullet, fired by one of the men, in the inner side of the right ankle.

They passed on through a footway at the south side of the Banbury Reservoir, thence northward through a narrow pathway towards Highham Hill. Here Sidney Charles Slater, age 30, a horse-keeper, out of work, of 6 Eaton Place, Fore Street, Edmonton rather recklessly followed these men into this footpath when the murderers fired 6 or 7 shots at him. He was hit in the left thigh and disabled. First Aid was rendered by Police and he was conveyed to Tottenham Hospital.

They crossed by the base of Higham Hill through some allotments. Frederick Easter, age 27, a single man, of 1 Billet Road, Higham Hill joined in the chase. When in Folly Lane the murderers turned and fired upon their pursuers and Easter was shot, the bullet striking him on the left thigh and passed through the fleshy part of his left leg. They now entered a field where (there) was a gipsy encampment in the same reckless way the miscreants fired amongst the gipsies, but fortunately without causing any hurt or damage. They now entered the premises of Salisbury Hall Farm and took temporary shelter behind a haystack. From either side of it they continuously fired upon the pursuers who were fully exposed to the deadly fire, many saving themselves by promptly lying down flat on the ground. It was during this severe encounter that William Roker, age 32, a labourer, married, of 4 Cross Street, Edmonton, was very severely injured being shot in both legs. He was promptly attended to and conveyed to the Walthamstow Cottage Hospital where he now lies in a critical condition.

The murderers now passed through the farm yard to the Chingford Road. Without a moment's hesitation, they commandeered an electric tram car en route to the Bakers Arms P. H. Lea Bridge Road. The driver and conductor were held up at the point of the revolver. The driver stopped the car and rushed upstairs leaving the conductor who was forced with the muzzle of the revolver at his head to go to the controller and drive them with all speed. Also at this point they were holding at bay a large crowd of pursuers. An old man named Edward Loveday, aged 63, of 2 Devonshire Villas, Hall Lane, Chingford, was a passenger. He made an attempt to leave the car when he was shot through the neck by one of the murderers. There was also a female passenger but she was unhurt. Loveday is an inmate of the Walthamstow Hospital and is progressing favourably. The conductor proceeded as far as the Victory P. H. St Johns Road, where there is a loop line. He reduced speed to allow a car coming in an opposite direction to pass him and then put on full speed to Kite's Corner. By a simple but ingenious ruse he got rid of his undesirable passengers by telling the man standing by him that the Police Station was just round the corner. This was effectual for he was directed to pull up and the men hurriedly left the car. Just here they commandeered a milk cart which was stationary. George Conyard, age 19, of Roase [sic] Cottage, Chingford Road who was inside a shop, seeing the horse being driven off rushed out to stop it, but he was immediately shot down, the bullet passing through his right arm and chest. He too is in Walthamstow

Hospital and progressing favourably. They drove up Farnham Avenue to Forest Road, Walthamstow. Here they were overtaken by a horse and van driven Thomas White, greengrocer, Chingford Road, Walthamstow. One of the men pointed a revolver at White's head and he jumped off his seat which the men took possession of and drove rapidly towards Wood Street.

PC 236 "N" Adams commandeered a motor car and followed, blowing his whistle and attracted the attention of PS Jowitt and PC 616 "N" Francis on duty at Hagger Bridge. These officers made on attempt to stop them when one of the men fired at them and the bullet passed between them and broke the glass panel of the side door of 849 Forest Road, occupied by Charles Pipe, a greengrocer.

The action of the officers diverted their course, they turned into Kingsley Road driving across waste land to Fulbourne Road to Wadham Road, thence into Winchester Road where they deserted the van and ran to the River Ching, through this part of the route Jacob was driving Helfeld possessed both revolvers and kept up a continuous fire upon the pursuers.

They clambered down the narrow bank of the River, Jacob succeeded in climbing the fence that bounds it, Helfeld attempted to do so but failed. He turned round and saw that his position was hopeless, he cried out to Jacob "Go on, save yourself, I've only got two left". He sank upon the ground and shot himself through the head. He was seized by Police, disarmed and taken as soon as possible to the Tottenham Hospital in a van requisitioned on the spot and he is now detained there under strict Police supervision. He is progressing very favourably and in a few days will be well enough to be charged.

Jacob was hotly pursued by PC 769 "N" Zeithing and was within a few yards of him when he turned and fired three shots at him, one of which passed over his left shoulder and entered the chest of Frederick John Mortimer, age 38, of 18 Palmerston Road, Walthamstow and came out at the back of him. This man had just thrown a brick at Jacob. The PC had a very narrow escape as one or more of the bullets passed through the lapels of his greatcoat. Mortimer is in Walthamstow Hospital and progressing very favourably.

Jacob had run on across Hale End Read into a field at the rear of Oak Cottage, Hale End, occupied by Charles Rolstone, a coal porter. Here he was lost sight of by everyone but as a matter of fact he had sought shelter in this small house, consisting of four rooms and a lean-to. He first ran to the front room, where judging from the amount of soot which was found lying in the room he had made an attempt to climb into the chimney. I may say that on entering the kitchen of this house he had peered through a small window in the door of the lean-to his face was covered with blood, no doubt caused by the small shot from the fowling pieces of men who had shot at him when crossing the fields in the earlier part of the chase. Mrs Rolstone saw him, screamed and ran out of the place, crying "Oh my children".

Jacob then shut and bolted that door also the front street door. Charles Schaffer, a baker, of 22 Carlton Road, Walthamstow, who had chased these men throughout went to the door of the lean to and with the assistance of PC 336 "N" Dewhurst burst it open both passed into the kitchen and brought the children out safely.

After failing in his attempt to hide in the parlour chimney, Jacob went upstairs into the front bedroom. He gave a stealthy look through the window which was seen by his pursuers who had now arrived in large numbers and some of whom were armed. They at once poured a volley in the direction, shattering most of the contents of the room.

At this Juncture PC 636 "J" Charles Eagles and PC Charles Dixon C.I.D and PC 714 "N" John Cater rendered good service The former obtained a ladder from adjoining premises and placed it against the back bedroom window. He obtained a loaded gun from a bystander, climbed the ladder, opened the window and looked in. PC Dixon had sent a dog up into this room which Eagles encouraged to go under the bed. At that moment he turned round and saw Jacob with the door of the front bedroom ajar pointing the revolver at him. He found that the gun was unworkable through a safety catch which he did not understand and rapidly descended the ladder. He changed the weapon for a Police revolver which PC Dixon was carrying. The three officers then climbed this very narrow staircase, Eagles being in front, Dixon in the centre and Cater behind. It was perfectly clear that if the miscreant secured the first shot that these men would have been seriously hurt or killed because it will be seen by the history of this case that Jacob was a dead shot. Eagles fired twice and Cater once through the panel of the door. Now there was a shot heard in the room by most people though these men though Eagles asserts that Jacob opened the door slightly and presented his revolver at him, but in the fearful excitement of the moment the PC could have believed this. Evidence has since proved that a Police shot did not despatch this man. He shot himself. Upon Police entering the room Jacob was found upon a small bed in the corner in the throes of death and immediately afterwards expired. The body was carried down into the yard and subsequently seen by Dr Alcock of Castle Avenue, Highams Park and Dr Wainwright, Divl. Surgeon of Tottenham. It was then conveyed on Police Ambulance to the Walthamstow Mortuary, Queens Road.

It has been identified as that of a Russian known as "Yacob" who has been employed at a furniture factory at Tottenham, owned by Messrs Lebus and Co. Helfeld was formerly employed by Mr Schnurmann but only for a few days. Enquiries as to their antecedents are in progress by the officers of Special Branch.

In addition to the injured persons named above the following also sustained personal injury:—

William Devine, age 13, of 145 Melbourne Road, Tottenham.
Shot in right leg.

George Harwood, age 26, of 6 Park Lane, Tottenham.
Wound of fore finger right hand, inflicted at the railway bridge supposed by Jacob, as he was making his escape.

George Rawson, age 40, of 9 Havelock Road, Tottenham.

Received a slight bullet wound on inner side of right wrist, when the murderers were firing from the bridge spanning the Mill Stream.

Joseph William Ayley, age 30, of 113 Love Lane, Tottenham.
A slight wound on left knee when rendering assistance to P.C Tyler.

George Cousins, age 29, of 14 Asplins Road, Tottenham.
Received a bullet in thick part of left shoulder, after lying down for a short time renewed the chase.

William Stephen Thomas Edwards, age 28, 4 Leeds Street, Edmonton.
Received a shot in the left elbow near where PC Tyler fell.

P.C 50 "N" Hawking[e]s graze over left eye and leg but how caused is not clear.
He was following the murderer in an advertisement cart. One of the murderers shot the pony causing it to fall and Hawking[e]s and the men with him were thrown out. Bullets had passed through the leg and seat of his trousers. He was armed with a gun but did not use it.

LIST OF POLICE INJURED FROM OTHER CAUSES.
CLIMBING FENCES ETC.

PC 513 "N" Forde sprain of left thigh.

PC 238 "N" Woadden lacerated thumb of right hand

PC 534 "N" Brown jagged wound of left hand.

PC 406 "N" Bond contracted a chill through taking up the chase partly dressed.

TOTAL NUMBER OF CASUALTIES   25.

The weapons used by these men were powerful up to date magazines and the bullets used were "expanding".

They had but few left when captured. I am glad to say that with the exception of Roker all the civilian patients who are of the labouring class are progressing favourably.

Upon Jacob there were found two paper bank bags, one of which contained £5 silver the other being empty. This would be the property of Mr Schnurmann.

This extraordinary man hunt was carried on over a course extending about six miles.

It would be impossible for me to speak too highly of the splendid conduct of the Police of "N" and "J" Divisions. In response to my call to duty they were most prompt and in action cool, tactful and fearless.

The conduct of the Public engaged was equally brave and praiseworthy.

The concluding observations I have to make are brief, simply that immediately on receiving the news and sending out directions to all stations on the division and Supt Dearn ("J") which afterwards found had been already done by officers at different on their initiative I drove to scene with my groom and a PC in plain clothes armed with a revolver and ammunition, taking a direct course to Woodford, that being the last place where I heard the murder[er]s were making for. When I reached the Napier Arms P. H. Woodford I was informed by Police scouts of the death (of) Jacob at the cottage near by and the arrest of Helfeld.

I preceded there and took general charge.

Sgd W. Jenkins
Superintendent

APPENDIX 2

Email from Helen MacDonald, Manager of the Carnegie Hero Fund Trust to the Author

20 July 2016

Dear Geoff,

The Carnegie Hero Fund Trust recognised the heroism of people who had been involved in The Tottenham Outrage and details which we have about the incident are as follows:

"What is known as the Tottenham Outrage, which took place on 23 January 1909, was the occasion of a number of instances of heroism. Two foreign desperadoes, armed with revolvers, robbed a clerk, and, in their efforts to escape capture, shot recklessly at their pursuers and at others who chanced to be in their way. A police officer and a boy were killed, and many, both of the police and citizens, were wounded. Many joined in the pursuit, and both among the police and among private persons there were cases in which conspicuous courage was shown in the efforts made to stop the career of the murderers. The Chief Commissioner of Police, after making careful investigation, prepared for the consideration of the Trustees a report, which contained all the cases which, in his opinion, were deserving of special notice. Six persons, some of whom had been more or less seriously injured, had acted with conspicuous courage, namely as George Smith; George Cousins; William G. Roker; Joseph Wilson; Charles Schaffer and H. G. North. Among the members of the police force who joined in the pursuit, the following had acted with exceptional gallantry, namely, Police Constables Nicod, Eagles, Dixon, Cater, Newman, Ziething, and Dewhurst. At the request of the Home Secretary, a committee was formed to raise a fund for the relief of private persons who had been wounded in connection with the pursuit of criminals. The committee found that nearly 20 persons were entitled to relief and it was expected that the sum of about £750 would be required for the purpose. The Trustees decided to contribute £100 to the fund. They further decided that a medallion should be presented to each of the seven police officers whose names were submitted by the Commissioner as deserving of special notice."

In addition to the award of bronze medallions, the names of those police officers mentioned above were entered in the Roll of Honour, a beautifully illustrated book that is displayed in the Andrew Carnegie Birthplace Museum here in Dunfermline. It contains the names of over 6,000 people whose heroism has been recognised by the Trustees since the foundation of the Hero Fund Trust in 1908. I attach a photograph of the opening pages of Volume 1 of the Roll and one of the entry in the officers' names.

We wish you success with your book and I hope this information helps with your research.

With kind regards,

Helen

Helen MacDonald
Manager, Carnegie Hero Fund Trust

APPENDIX 3

Route of the Chase

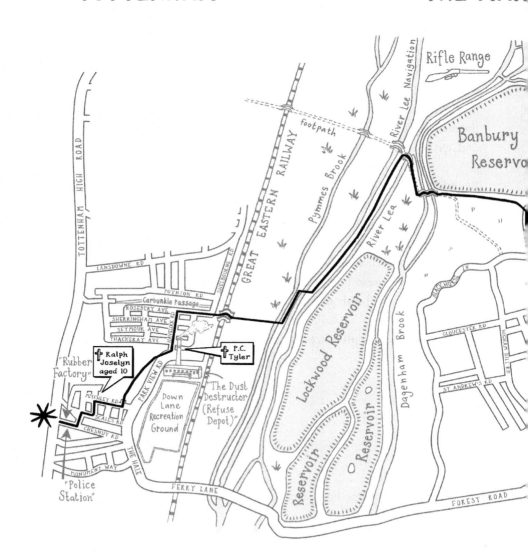

HES

WALTHAMSTOW

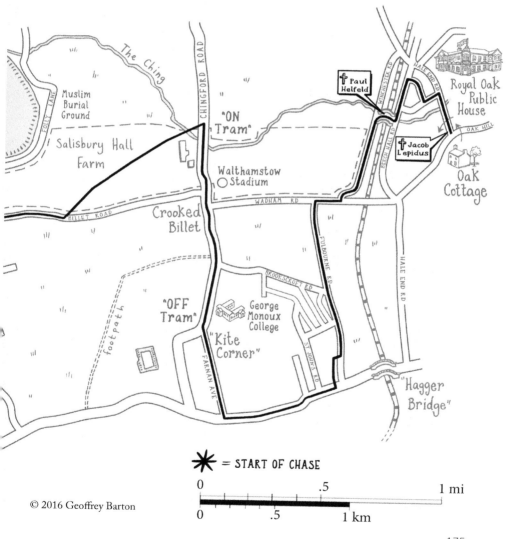

✳ = START OF CHASE

0 — .5 — 1 mi

0 — .5 — 1 km

Tottenham High Road.

Chesnut Road (the scene of the robbery).

Chesnut Grove.

Scales Road.

Dawlish Road.

Mitchley Road (where Ralph Joscelyne was shot).

Junction Road.

Across fields that are now Holcombe Road/Buller Road/Mafeking Road and Carew Road.

Dowsett Road.

Down Lane (now Park View Road) (around here PC Tyler was shot: dying he was then taken to Oak Cottage in Thackeray Avenue).

Across Down Lane Crossing (the footbridge into the Marshes).

Past Milmead Industrial Centre and the Allotments.

Crossing Pymme's Brook.

North on the west side of the River Lea Navigation (the canal) as it runs close and parallel to the west bank of Lockwood Reservoir.

Crossing the River Lea Navigation at Stonebridge Lock.

Running north-east between the Navigation and the River Lea.

Crossing the River Lea at Chalk Bridge.

Past the Rifle Range and the Butts, now the Hastingwood Trading Estate and the Lea Valley Trading Estate.

Running around Banbury Reservoir, anti-clockwise from due west to due south.

Ching Brook.

Mill Stream Bridge.

Folly Lane.

Billet Road at the edge of the area known as Higham Hill.

Salisbury Hall Farm (later Walthamstow Stadium).

Crooked Billet Roundabout.

Chingford Road, where the robbers took over the tram.

Kite's Corner (Chingford Road and Farnham Road) (where the robbers abandoned the tram and took over a milk cart).

Farnham Road.

Forest Road (where the robbers abandoned the milk cart and took over a greengrocer's cart).

Hagger Bridge (Forest Road between Fulborne Road and Hale End Road).

Fulbourne Road.

Wadham Road.

Winchester Road.

Kingsley Road.

Beech Hall Road.

Prestons Avenue (where the robbers abandoned the greengrocer's cart).

River Ching (where Helfeld shot himself).

Hale End Road.

Royal Oak Public House.

Oak Cottage (where Lepidus was trapped and shot himself, and the incident finally ended).

APPENDIX 4

The Cast[2]

Police Officers involved in the chase

1. Superintendent Jenkins
2. Chief Inspector Holland
3. Divisional Detective Inspector Martin
4. Inspector Gould
5. Sub-Divisional Inspector Haines
6. Sub-Divisional Inspector Large
7. Station Sergeant Hart
8. Police Sergeant (CID) Haigh
9. Police Sergeant 7 "N" Hale
10. Police Sergeant Howitt
11. Police Sergeant 67 "N" Jowitt
12. Police Sergeant 44 "N" Mackay
13. Detective Constable Charles Dixon
14. Police Constable (PC) 236 "N" Adams
15. PC 288 "N" Baldwin
16. PC 222 "J" Bleadon
17. PC 406 "N" Bond
18. PC 853 "N" Brewer
19. PC 534 "N" Brown PC Byrne
20. PC 153 "N" Commerford
21. PC 714 "N" John William Cater
22. PC Cutler
23. PC 336 "N" Dewhurst
24. PC Dixon
25. PC 636 "J" Charles Eagles
26. PC Field
27. PC 513 "N" Forde
28. PC 637 "N" Fraiser
29. PC 616 "N" Francis
30. PC Gibb
31. PC 50 "N" Hawking[e]s
32. PC 755 "N" Lawrence

---

2. Based on MPS papers held in The National Archives.

33. PC Lewis
34. PC Martin
35. PC McLean
36. PC 510 "N" Albert Newman
37. PC 313 "N" William Henry Nicod
38. PC Rushbrook
39. PC 747 "N" Shakespeare
40. PC Spedding
41. PC 403 "N" William Tyler (deceased)
42. PC Vine
43. PC Wadley
44. PC Willard
45. PC Williams
46. PC 807 "N" Willison
47. PC 442 "J" Wilson
48. PC 238 "N" Woadden
49. PC 789 "N" Alexander E Ziething

Members of the Public known to have been involved in the chase

1. Dr Allcock
2. Charles Allison (16)
3. Mrs Elizabeth Andrews
4. Joseph William Ayley (Aka Bayley)
5. Frederick Baker
6. Thomas Brown
7. Cyril Burgess
8. Paul Casewitz
9. Mrs May Cawley
10. George Conyard
11. George Cousins
12. Mr Cubley
13. William Devine (Aka Denny)
14. William Dormer
15. Frederick Easter
16. Mr William Stephen Thomas Edwards
17. Mr Fowler
18. Walter Green
19. Mrs Green
20. George Harwood
21. Ralph John Joscelyne (deceased) (age 10)
22. Edward Loveday
23. Albert Keyworth (17)
24. Frederick John Mortimer
25. Frederick Perry (17)

26. Charles Pipe
27. George Rawson
28. William Roker
29. Charles Rolstone
30. Mrs Eliza Rolstone
31. Master Rolstone (age 12)
32. Master Charles Rolstone (age 6)
33. Master Rolstone (age 3)
34. Charles Schaffer
35. Julius Schnurmann
36. Robert Skinner
37. Sidney Charles Slater
38. Joseph Slow
39. George Smith
40. Mrs Spedding
41. Victor Albert Tolley
42. Thomas White
43. Wilkinson
44. Frederick Williams
45. Arthur Wilmot
46. Joseph Wilson
47. Woods
48. Charles Wyatt

Casualties

The official report lists seven wounded Police Officers and 17 wounded civilians. Lists of police and civilian casualties are always distorted by the fact that every police officer reports every injury, however minor, because he is compelled to do so by legislation. If PC Bond had felt the need to take a day off work and stay in bed to recover from his chill, and had not reported it, then he would be guilty of an offence. A civilian would not have had a problem if he had not reported it.

Police:

PC 403 "N" Tyler — Deceased.

PC 406 "N" Bond — Lacerated hand and contracted chill from leaving the police station partly dressed.

PC 534 "N" Brown — Jagged wound to hand.

PC 513 "N" Forde — Sprain of left thigh.

PC 50 "N" Hawkings — Graze over left eye and to leg and two bullets passed through the leg and seat of his trousers.

PC 510 "N" Newman — Graze on his cheek and wound on lobe of right ear during road traffic accident as bullet grazed right cheek.

PC 313 "N" Nicod — Shot in his left thigh and leg.

PC 238 "N" Woadden — Lacerated thumb of right hand.

Civilians:

Ralph Joscelyne, ten-year-old schoolboy — Deceased.

Mr Joseph William Bayley (also referred in this and some other sources as Ayley), general dealer, 113 Love Lane, Tottenham — Shot in right knee while rendering assistance to PC Tyler.

Mr Cyril Burgess, aged 16, Wickham Road, Tottenham — Bullet wound in leg inner side of right ankle at the same time as PC Nicod.

Mr George Conyard, aged 19, milkman, Rose Cottage, Chingford — Shot in the chest and arm when Helfeld and Jacob stole his milk cart.

Mr George Cousins, aged 29, casual market porter 14 Asplins Road, Tottenham. Married with three dependent children — Bullet in left shoulder but resumed chase after lying down for a short time.

William Devine (also referred in some sources as Denny), aged 13, Welbourne Road, Tottenham — Shot in right leg.

Mr Frederick Easter, aged 27, bricklayer, 1 Billet Road, Higham Hill. Single, supporting his mother — Shot in left thigh while pursuing Helfeld and Jacob at Folly Lane.

Mr William Stephen Thomas Edwards, aged 28, Leeds Road, Edmonton — Shot in left elbow near where PC Tyler fell.

Mr George Harwood, aged 26, labourer, 6 Park Lane, Tottenham. Married with one dependent child — Fingers of right hand wounded at railway bridge, allegedly by Jacob as he was making his escape.

Mr Edward Loveday, aged 63, glass merchant, 2 Devonshire Villas, Hall Lane, Chingford Mount — Shot in the throat.

Mr Frederick Mortimer, aged 38, master plasterer, 18 Palmerstone Road, Walthamstow. Married with seven dependent children — Shot in the chest on both sides.

Mr George Rawson, aged 40, 9 Havelock Road, Tottenham — Slight bullet wound to inner side of right wrist from where Helfeld and Jacob were firing from midstream bridge.

Mr William Roker, aged 32, unemployed plasterer's labourer, 4 Cross Street, Angel Road, Edmonton. Married with three dependent children — Shot in both legs at Salisbury Hall Farm.

Mr Sidney Slater, aged 30, unemployed horse keeper, 6 Eaton Place, Fore Street, Edmonton. Married with six dependent children — Shot in left thigh near Higham Hill.

Mr George Smith, aged 40, gas stoker, 17 Hartington Road, Tottenham. Married with six dependent children — Grazed by bullets when attempting to detain Helfeld and Jacob.

Mr Thomas Williams or (William Thomas), aged 28 Leeds Street, Edmonton — Bullet wound to left elbow near where PC Tyler fell.

Arthur Wilmot, aged 15, 69 Scales Road, Tottenham — Bullet wound to elbow.

Mr Joseph Wilson, aged 29, chauffeur to Mr Schnurmann, 22 West Hampstead Mews, Hampstead — Grazed by bullets while pursuing Helfeld and Jacob.

…And one injured horse!

APPENDIX 5

Letter from the Russian Consulate[3]

Imperial Russian Consulate General
London
No 323

Windsor Chambers,
20, Great St Helens, E.C.

1st February 1909

To The Chief Commissioner of the Metropolitan Police
New Scotland Yards, SW.

Dear sir,

I have the honour of requesting you to arrange that the wreath that I send you may be placed on the grave of the fearless Police Officer who fell a victim of the recent Tottenham Outrage. In doing so I wish to show my admiration for the London Metropolitan Police Force, to which the deceased belonged, and my sincere sympathy with the bereaved. The murderer, who is said to be a Russian subject was not a Russian speaking ethnographically.

I am, sir

Yours very truly,

Consul General.

---

3.   Source: MPS/National Archives.

APPENDIX 6

Statement of Thomas William Brown[4]

Thomas William Brown
11, Albion Road,
Forest Road,
Walthamstow.

On January 23 1909 I heard my son, Thomas calling out, "Dad come quick." I saw him running down Kingsley Road and then a PC named Adams running down Forest Road. He said, "Don't go too near; they have shooters." I still kept running down Kingsley Road, and then I saw two men in a van the one driving whilst the other was at the tailboard with a revolver in each hand and he fired at me, the bullet whizzing past my right temple. I was still pursuing when one of them fired at me again and this time the bullet passed through the right leg of my trousers. I still continued in the chase following the murderers down Fulbourne Road they were still firing at random on their pursuers. They then turned to the left down Brookscroft Road, still firing until they reached Beresford Road. After this they turned into Wadham Road. Then I went around into Chingford Road. Here I met a PC who was doing point duty. I said, "Come with me quick. The murderers are up here meaning Winchester Road. He and another PC came running with me and then we saw a motorcar that was in pursuit. Into this we all got; also a gentleman who happened to arrive with a breech-loading gun in his possession. We proceeded down the Wadham Road as quickly as possible and whilst on the way we were firing at our assail-ants. Soon the gentleman in possession of the breech-loading gun left the car and let me have the use of the gun and some cartridges. I fired at our assailants in Wadham Road and the tallest (sic) of the two murderers who

---

4. Source: MPS/National Archives.

held a revolver in each hand was keeping a furious fire on us all the time. Soon they were into Winchester Road, Highams Park. Here Mr North and myself fired on the two men in the van. Shortly they abandoned the van and commenced a retreat on foot. I then noticed the tallest (sic) of the two hand his mate one of the two weapons he had been using and then made off for a fence that was close by. Here it was that Mr North and myself fired at the tallest (sic) of the two. He fell this side of the fence and was then seen to turn his revolver on himself, shooting himself in the right temple. I then ran on with two PCs, one of them picked up the revolver that had been used by the assassin. I asked the PC 747 for the revolver. We then continued to chase the murder who was now alone. He made his way across to a place called Beech Hall Estate. Here they were erecting some houses, and more shots were fired by the assailant now at large and a plasterer by the name of F. Mortimer was shot in the right breast. The he (sic) ran across Oak Hill, through the hedge, across the back of the Oak Public House towards Oak Cottages, I then reloaded the gun I had with me. Then I saw our assailant creeping behind the hedges with his revolver in his left hand, and he saw me taking aim at him. Then he made for one of the cottages nearby and admitted himself by the back way. Soon I saw him at one of the bedroom windows. Then I fired at him, the shot piercing some of the windows of the room. The detective Nixon came through the house and said, "Don't fire any more for God's sake as there are 3 or 4 of us inside now. I then entered the house and heard Nixon shout up the stairs to the assailant to surrender, but no answer came. By this PC Eagles was firing up the stairs at the door and soon all was quiet for some seconds. Then a loud report rang out and Inspector Gould of Tottenham made for the room. I then following Nixon and PC Eagles. I then saw a man lying on a bed bleeding from a wound in the right temple and a revolver laying on the bed by his side.

[Living as he did, in Walthamstow, there is no reason to believe that Mr Brown would have known the police officers from Tottenham before the incident. Therefore, presumably the Detective Nixon that he refers to in his statement is the Detective Dixon referred to by the other witnesses as being at the cottage].

APPENDIX 7

Statement of Henry George North[5]

"On Saturday, January 23rd last, about 11:30 am, I was in Forest Road serving my customers from my horse and van, when I heard a lot of police whistles blowing. On looking round, I saw two men in a horse and van coming towards me; one of the men was driving, the other stood at the back part of the van. Following them was a crowd of police and civilians shouting: *'Stop them, men!'*

I left serving my customers and went into the middle of the road, and tried to stop the horse as I did so to get hold of the reins. The man who was driving pointed a revolver at me and fired, but missed me. I ran to my van and, picking up a two-pound weight, gave chase after them. I caught up to them at the top of Spruce Hill Road, when the man at the back part of the van pointed his revolver at me; at the same time, I got behind a van that was coming in the opposite direction. I again caught up to them at the corner of Kingsly Road, where they both fired at some police; at that time, I threw my weight at them.

I followed them down Kingsly Road and across a field; they fired at me three or four times, then I got into a motor car and the gentleman who sat in it handed me a gun and some cartridges. We caught up to them again at Wadham Road School and down Billet Lane where I had a shot at them and

When they got down Winchester Road, they both left the horse and van, and made for a fence that runs along the railway. The man that had been driving got over; the other one walked a few paces along the fence and tried

---

5. Henry North's statement to the MPS made at the time of The Outrage was never used or retained by them. It later found its way into the hands of Patricia Collier and was reproduced in her monograph *Secrets of the Tottenham Outrage* (2007).

to get over; when he was at the top of the fence, I fired, and he fell. I then jumped into the river and got up the other side, climbed over the fence, and a man handed me the gun over, and then I went after the other man who I could see running across a field.

I chased him until we came to some houses being built. There were several workmen leaving off work, and at that time the man who I was chasing turned and fired several shots. A man who was just at my side put his hand to his side and shouted: *'Oh, take it out! Oh, my poor wife and children!'* I did not stop to render him any assistance, but kept on after the man. He got over a gate into a field and walked along the hedge, loading his revolver as he went. I got alongside a tree and had a shot at him; he stopped and fired at me, then he ran away and I lost sight of him.

I ran along the road to a public house; the landlord, who had heard the shots, came out to see what the matter was. I told him there was a murderer about: he ran indoors and bolted them. I then ran along the front of some cottages and saw a woman and two little children standing at the gate of one of them. I told her to go inside as there was a murderer about; I went to the end of these cottages but, as 1 could not see the man, I came back again. Then, I again saw this woman standing outside the cottage, and someone said: *"He is in there!"* pointing to the cottage. I ran up the path and stood at the door with my gun ready.

A man afterwards came up and burst the door open, and got the two children out; very soon, the police arrived and we searched the bottom part of the place, but could not find anybody there. *We* went to the back, and someone said: 'He *is upstairs';* we stood at the bottom of the stairs, and after several shots had been fired, the police and myself rushed upstairs and saw the man lying on the bed dead, with a bullet wound in his temple. I helped to carry him downstairs, and afterwards, 1 went with Superintendent Jenkins and identified the man shot alongside me, who 1 knew as Mortimer, also the man I shot at on the fence, as one of the men who was in the horse and van.

I then walked back to Forest Road where I had left my horse and van, and was told that it had been taken home by a Mr. Wignell of Wood Street, because the children had been stealing the fruit from it. Although I was in such an exhausted condition, I again went on my round to serve my customers, but the shock had been too much for me, and I went home, leaving my round unfinished."

Police statement given to Patricia Collier.

APPENDIX 8

Statement of Mrs Eliza Rolstone[6]

Eliza Rolstone, who lived in a cottage at Oak Hill, at Oak Cottage in Oak Hill, where the chase ended when Jacob Lepidus shot himself, gave this description of events:

"I was standing in my garden when I heard police whistles and a constable came running along, shouting to people to close all their doors. *"There is a murderer about,"* he shouted. I turned towards my cottage and was surprised to see that the door had been closed. I have a lean-to shed as part of my kitchen and saw that the door of this had also been fastened.

I looked through a hole in the door and saw, to my horror, the bloodstained face of a desperate man, with wild-looking eyes. I screamed in horror, for in the kitchen I had left my two little boys."

Statement given to Patricia Collier.

---

6. MPS/National Archives/Collier (see note to *Appendix 7*).

APPENDIX 9

Return of Claims Made After The Outrage[7]

23rd February 1909

"N" or Islington Division

RETURN showing names of persons who made claims for compensation
FOR LOSS OR DAMAGE TO PROPERTY, either from the action of
the assailants or after being placed at the use of the pursuers voluntarily
and for loss of employment due to same.

---

7. Source: The National Archives.

Name and address	Age	Married or single and the no. of depend. children	Occupation	How many days in hospital and if still there	Period from injury until likely to resume work	Wages per week usually earned	How much wages lost up to date from 23.1.09	Likely loss of wages before resuming work	Amount claimed for loss/ damage to property.	Nature of damage to property	Total amount of claim		
George Smith, 17 Hartington Road, Tottenham.	40	Married 6	Gas stoker (works on Sundays)	Treated as an out patient	Not worked since 13th inst but will resume 1st prox	£2.4.0	Nil	£4.16.0	£2	Damage to clothing by bullet holes and blood.	6	16	0
George Cousins, 14 Asplins Road, Tottenham.	31	Married 3	Market porter (casual)	Treated as an out patient.	3 days	£1.10.0	150d	Nil	120d	Overcoat, Guernsey and two shirts damaged by bullets.	1	7	0
William Geo Roker, 4 Cross Street, Edmonton.	30	Married 3	Plasterer's labourer	32 days and still there	10 weeks	£1.18.0	£8.4.8	£10.15.4	105d	Trousers spoilt by bullet holes, blood and cutting.	19	10	0
Sidney Chas Slater, 6 Eaton Place, Edmonton	30	Married 6	Horse keeper	25 days	10 weeks	£1.6.0	£5.12.8	£7.7.4	£1	Overcoat, trousers and pants perforated with bullets and damaged by blood.	14	0	0
George Harwood, 6 Park Lane, Tottenham.	26	Married 1	Labourer	Treated as an out patient	5 weeks and 1 day.	£1.6.0	£5.12.8	£1.1.8	550d	Overcoat torn during chase by barbed wire	6	19	4

Name and address	Age	Married or single and the no. of depend. children	Occupation	How many days in hospital and if still there	Period from injury until likely to resume work	Wages per week usually earned	How much wages lost up to date from 23.1.09	Likely loss of wages before resuming work	Amount claimed for loss/ damage to property.	Nature of damage to property	Total amount of claim		
Frederick John Mortimer, 18 Palmerston Road, Walthamstow.	38	Married 7	Master plasterer	32 days and still there	10 weeks	£3 15.0	£16 5.0	£21 5.0	£2	Coat, vest and two shirts damaged by bullets and blood	39	10	0
William S.T. Edwards 4 Leeds Street, Edmonton.	28	Married 3	Builder's labourer	Treated as an out patient	6 weeks	£1 10.0	£6 10.0	£2 10.0	£1 6.0	Overcoat and jacket perforated by bullets	10	6	0
Joseph Wm Ayley, 113 Love Lane, Tottenham.	36	Married 3	Dealer	Not medically treated	Nil	£1.5.0	45s6d	Nil	10s0d	Old pair of trousers perforated by bullets and rags etc. lost from barrow.	14	14	2
William Fredk Devine, 145 Welbourne Road, Tottenham.	13	—	Schoolboy	Treated as an out-patient	Convalescent	—	—	—	7s6d	Trousers, drawers and stockings spoilt by perforation and blood	7	7	6
Lizzie Green, Gate House, Downs Lane, Tottenham.	45	Married 4	Husband a platelayer	Privately treated	2 days	—	—	—	50s0d	Two days aid in work in consequence of shock	1	0	0

Name and Address	Age	Condition	Occupation	Treatment	Duration	Amount	Amount	Amount	Claim	Remarks	£	s	d
Cyril John Burgess, 65, Wycombe Road, Tottenham.	16	Single	Electrician	Treated as an out-patient and privately	7 weeks	10s0d	£2.10.0	£1	£1.6.0 2s6d	For medical attendance Trousers and socks perforated by bullets	4	18	6
Frederick Easter, 1 Billet Road, Walthamstow.	27	Single	Bricklayer	Privately treated	14 days	£1 15 0	£3.10.0	--	7s6d 10s6d	For medical attendance Trousers damaged by shot holes and blood.			
Edward Loveday, 2 Devonshire Villas, Hall Lane, Chingford.	63	Married 0	Glass silverer	24 days	Very indefinite	£2.15.0	£11.18.4	Very indefinite	£1.10.0 £1.1.0	Trousers and vest spoilt with blood. Bag lost in tram car.			
George Sidney Conyard, Rose Cottage, Chapel End, Walthamstow.	19	Single	Farm labourer	32 days and still there	9 weeks	£1.0.0	£4.6.8	£4.13.4	£2.15.0	Suits, pants, 2 shirts and a pair of boots spoilt by blood and cutting.	11	15	0
Joseph Wilson, 22 West Hampstead Mews, Hampstead.	29	Married 1	Chauffeur	Not injured	--	£2.10.0	Nil	Nil	£2	Overcoat, under-coat, 2 vests and two shirts perforated by bullets in many places.	2	0	0
Charles Wyatt, 47, Selbourne Road, Walthamstow.	--	Married	Tram conductor	Not injured	--	--	Nil	Nil	10s6d	Boot damaged and golosh torn off by bullet.		10	6

Name and address	Age	Married or single and the no. of depend. children	Occupation	How many days in hospital and if still there	Period from injury until likely to resume work	Wages per week usually earned	How much wages lost up to date from 23.1.09	Likely loss of wages before resuming work	Amount claimed for loss/ damage to property.	Nature of damage to property	Total amount of claim
Thomas W. Brown, 11, Albion Road, Walthamstow.	–	Married	Greengrocer	Not injured	–	–	Nil	Nil	12s6d	Trousers damaged by bullets.	12 6
F. Thorogood, Oak Villa, Thackeray Road, Tottenham.	–	Married	Railway guard	Not injured	–	–	Nil	Nil	£1.10.0	Table cloths and carpet spoiled with blood. PC Tyler was taken in this house for first aid attention.	1 10 0
Charles Pipe, 849 Forest Road, Walthamstow.	–	Married	Greengrocer	Not injured	Nil	–	–	–	2s6d	Glass panel of door broken by bullet.	2 6
John Westley, Butchers Cottage, Chingford Road, Walthamstow.	–	Married	Haddock smoker	Not injured	Nil	–	–	–	1sod	Pane of glass in window broken by bullet.	1 0
Ferdinand Reius, St Juliens, Hampstead Road, Walthamstow.	–	–	Electrical engineer	Not injured	Nil	–	–	–	£1.1.0	Wings of motor car damaged by pursuers hanging on. It was lent to Police.	1 1 0

Name and Address	Age	Condition	Occupation	Nature of Injury						Amount	Particulars of Claim	£	s.	d.
Walthamstow District Council.	—	—	—	—	—	—	—	—	—	£2.1.0	Glass and a switch broken by bullets.	2	1	0
Thomas White, Chingford Road, Walthamstow.	21	Single	Greengrocer	Not injured	—	Nil	—	—	—	£2.10.0	Overstrain to pony seized by murderers and used by Police to convey injured to hospital.	2	10	0
A.T. Rowntree, West Green School, Tottenham.	—	—	School-master	Not injured	—	Nil	—	—	—	3s9d	For damage to bicycle lent to Police.		3	9
Julius Schurmann, Chesnut Road, Tottenham.	—	Married	Rubber factor	Not injured	—	Nil	—	—	—	£15.0.0	Damage to glass screens, cushions, hood and radiator of motor car by bullets, lent to police.	15	0	0
Charles Rolstone, Oak Cottage, Hale End.	—	Married	Coal porter	Not injured	—	Nil	—	—	—	£10	Damage to the furniture.	10	0	0
Alfred W. Charlton, Black Dog P.H., Twickenham.	—	—	Licensed victualler	Not injured	—	Nil	—	—	—	£5	Damage to Oak Cottage	5	0	0

Name and address	Age	Married or single and the no. of depend. children	Occupation	How many days in hospital and if still there	Period from injury until likely to resume work	Wages per week usually earned	How much wages lost up to date from 23.1.09	Likely loss of wages before resuming work	Amount claimed for loss/damage to property.	Nature of damage to property	Total amount of claim		
William and Alfred Aldred, 10 Longfellow Road, Walthamstow.	--	--	Carme	Not injured	Nil	--	--	--	£16.2.0	Damage to van pony shot in leg and incidental charges in connection. Corrs89451/7.	16	2	0
George Rawson, 9 Havelock Road, Tottenham.	40	Married 1	Fireman	Nil	Nil	--	--	--	50d	For medical attendance to slight bullet wound on wrist.		5	0
Dr Rogers On behalf of Mr May, Hale End.	--	--	--	--	--	--	--	--	£7.7.0 Corr No 589764	Memo. Board considers the claim prior to date of receiving shock spoken of should not be entertained.	7	7	0
Supt Jenkins, N Division.	--	--	--	--	--	--	--	--	£5.10.0	As per a/c attached.	5	10	0
James Powell, Hoe Street, Walthamstow.	--	--	Jobmaster						50d	As per a/c attached and vide 589451/7		5	0

Signed
W.Jenkins
Superintendent

Select References

Collier, P (2007), *Secrets of the Tottenham Outrage*, N2 Visual Communications. ISBN: 978-0-955865-20-6.

Eastwood, C (2014), *Edwardian Gun Crime and the Tottenham Outrage of 1909*, Amazon Media. ASIN: B00I9XICWS.

Harris, J D (2000), *Outrage: An Edwardian Tragedy*, London: Wilson Harris Publications. ISBN: 978-0-953964-10-9.

Police Firearms Officers Association website: www.pfoa.co.uk/193/the-tottenham-outrage (Last accessed 1 July 2016).

The Tottenham Outrage: A Brief Excerpt www.walthamstowmemories.net/pdfs/BarryRyder-TottOutrage.pdf (Last accessed 1 July 2016).

Index

The Killing of Constable Keith Blakelock:
The Broadwater Farm Riot
Tony Moore
With a Foreword by Clive Emsley

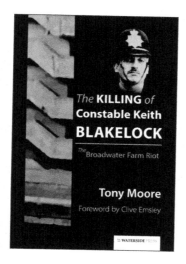

A closely observed account by someone working at senior level in the Met at the time. Deals with the biggest breakdown in community relations and law and order in modern English social and policing history. Looks at the entire sequence of events from their first rumblings to their aftermath and legacy.

'A remarkable book, not easy-reading yet easy to read, it is not for the faint-hearted and anyone who has policed in such dire circumstances may well be moved to tears... It should be compulsory reading not only for public order trainers and commanders but all senior officers. **It is highly recommended**' *Police History Society newsletter.*

Paperback & Ebook | ISBN 978-1-909976-20-7 | 2015 | 296 pages

www.WatersidePress.co.uk

Lightning Source UK Ltd.
Milton Keynes UK
UKOW05f2148030117
291285UK00005B/500/P